Worst Thing Best Thing

Bipolar Journey from Mental Health Client to Mental Health Professional

Cheryl Roma Yarek

ISBN 978-1-64349-414-2 (paperback)
ISBN 978-1-64349-416-6 (digital)

Christian Faith Publishing, Inc.
832 Park Avenue
Meadville, PA 16335
www.christianfaithpublishing.com

Toastmasters International and all other Toastmasters International trademarks and copyrights are the sole property of Toastmasters International. This book is the opinion of the author and is independent of Toastmasters International. It is not authorized by, sponsored by, affiliated with, or otherwise approved by Toastmasters International.

This is a true story; some names have been changed as requested by some individuals when queried. Some additional name changes are at the discretion of the author.

Printed in the United States of America

Dedicated to God with thanks for His constant presence.

I waited patiently for the Lord;
And He inclined to me and heard my cry.
He brought me up out of the pit of destruction,
out of the miry clay;
And He set my feet upon a rock making my
footsteps firm.
And He put a new song in my mouth,
a song of praise to our God;
Many will see and fear,
and trust in the Lord.
(Psalm 40:1–4)
Those who sow in tears
shall reap with joyful shouting.
(Psalm 126:5)
(From the Holy Bible)

With warmest thanks to Anne-Marie Vecchiarino
(my counsellor), who insisted I write my story and then read
it as it unfolded over time, page by page by page . . .

Childhood

"Cheril! Turn around and face the front! Cheril! Fermez la bouche!"

French language teacher, 1966

My father would appear each morning to say his prayers in the kitchen. It was there he had his pictures and icons of Jesus which he would kneel before. He completed his prayers every day with the same words, "Thank you, God, for another day of living." I would roll my seven-year-old eyes and think, *Man, he's annoying.* My father, using my nickname, would cheerfully ask, "Isn't it great to be alive, Chebbie?"

"Yeah, great," I would reply with sarcasm.

My mother, in remembering my childhood, explained, "We tried to direct you, to tell you what to do. You just kept doing what you wanted. I think you were three at the time, or maybe you were two and a half."

Until I started kindergarten and was corrected, I thought we might be Americans. My father admired no one more than the Americans. He would watch *The Fireside Chat* on TV, applaud throughout, and repeat constantly, "That's our president! That's our president!" (My parents and later myself travelled extensively in the States.) In childhood, my parents went there every summer, leaving me and my brother at my grandparents' farms. I used to miss them so much. I would wait for their return, sitting in the front yard on a lawn chair—every day in August. When they pulled in, I was never more excited. Tanned and smelling American, Mom would kiss me, and Dad would tuck me under a flowered arm. As we walked, I would cautiously leap to miss the toes of his new white shoes. My

7

parents were back from America, the land of little presents where the president spoke on TV and kind, lightly brown people sent rockets to the moon.

When I think of childhood, I remember my mother's optimism and my father's critical style, obsessive organizational skills, and doses of pessimism. Naturally, now from my vantage point as an adult who has spent many years in therapy, I name these things with a comfort I never felt as a child. And I view them with eyes wide open, intentionally kind, and accepting. I knew I adored my mother and was sometimes frightened of my father. It took many years for my father to recognize the dark effect of his occasional harshness. Myself, I have forgiven my father completely, mostly because I have made a great deal of mistakes myself—some serious.

My mother did try, always, to redirect. Her interventions were pleasant, like her. First, we would travel by streetcar to Simpson's, for a Vernors pop and an ice-cream waffle. Then hours at Eaton's, wandering and pondering, followed by a lunch of fish and chips and lemon ice-box cake. My mother balanced my propensity to negativity. When bad things happened, she was the best person to talk to. The phrase she repeated the most? "There is nothing so bad that something good does not come of it."

Many years later, my friend Sandy, and I would be talking on Facebook. She was with the Canadian Ethnic Media Association, and since I commented on our common Ukrainian background, she invited me to a gala. My reply was, "Actually, Sandy, I am a Canadian Ukrainian Polish German Jew. There was a lot of conflict in my family and tons of love, honesty, and ethics. We adored Florida and the Almond Bark at Laura Secord's, and speaking of *that*, sometimes we were just plain nuts!"

As a child, I was very smart and controlled by an overcritical father. My dad ran the show, and that included my life. Once he remarked, "In this house, my word is the law." Trust me, you would only test him once on it! Why? There was no argument. He was with the sheriff's department and drove a marked car. (No, I'm not kidding.)

My father had my high school courses, my university days, and my career planned before I was eight and without any input from me. He chose dentistry for me. My reply: "Great! I get to pick in people's mouths for the rest of my life!" Science and math were my worst subjects. I failed math three times in high school and went to summer school three times. Still, no relenting. I excelled at English, where I wrote depressing poems in my room (and during detentions), sometimes about my life as a prisoner of my father's ambitions for me. I loved the public library, one of the few places I was permitted to frequent. I was also very adept at history.

Even as a child, I remember thinking that my dad only represented the opinions of one man. I had a lot of very positive role models around me—four uncles, numerous male teachers, friends of my grandparents, and the Americans (our relatives from Illinois, Michigan, and West Virginia). One of the Americans, Ziggy, was my parents' age and especially fond of me. I was his dance partner at some weddings. Despite the fact that I stepped on his toes a lot, Ziggy's judgement was small and his heart, large. Mr. Harrison was another hero in my young life. As my grade 7 teacher, he spent one afternoon moving throughout various classrooms with me in hand because some guy had given me several punches at a red light during lunch. Mr. Harrison was going to find this guy and did. He said he could not accept anyone doing this to me, *especially* since I was in his "top ten" and read at a grade 13 level.

My early life revolved around my two sets of grandparents and my cousins. My paternal grandfather we referred to as Gi-Gi, and my grandmother was Ba-Ba. Gi-Gi ate his meals apart from the family although in the same dining room. His meals were served to him by Ba-Ba on a wooden cutting board that opened from the wall so that he could effectively control the room. He would give you a spoon, and you could share his soup on a Sunday afternoon, listening to Ukrainian voices on the radio.

As a child, I felt tormented at times. There were sometimes critical thoughts in my head making me feel imprisoned and condemned. I cried a lot, and my dad was intolerant of this. I also sketched, painted, and wrote every chance I had. One of my earliest poems was this:

Life

Life is but a moment,
a breathe in a game to play,
where nothing is totally given,
and memories fill hearts in a day.
Where dreams are lost in realness,
and mountains are too many to climb,
where money is hard to conceive,
and people still beg for a dime.
Life is haunting imaginings,
of things that never were,
where the past, the present, and future,
can be summed in one short word.
Life is wanting something,
too far from your grasp and reach.
Life is a legendary story,
no person or book can teach.

(Cheryl Yarek, 1969)

Before I left grade school, I was defending one of the kids from the bullies. I was not as tough as I pretended to be, but I was calculating. One of the bullies let me know I was going to get it for defending a vulnerable student. "Wait until after school, Yarek," she remarked. "We're going to beat the s——— out of you!"

"Oh . . ." I faltered. "After school, *where* exactly?"

"The front doors, right out here!" She pointed. (After school, I waited until they had all gathered at the front doors. I then made my exit out the rear doors at the very back of the school and speeded home.) By Monday, they had forgotten about it; I learned that these particular bullies had notoriously poor memories.

One day, a solution to my father's career pressure occurred to me. I would become a nun. I was attending Loretto Brunswick College School, so I made an appointment to speak to Sister Helen, whom I had an amazing rapport with. She said a decision like this was the result of a conversation with God, and when she learned there had been no conversation, she was not impressed. "You cannot hide in the convent from your father," she announced. Then she added, "There is only one way. You have to tell him you won't be a dentist." While she looked at me in a serious way, I was imagining explosions and some sort of event that would clearly lead to a major catastrophe. It seemed inevitable and the only way out.

We went to church every Sunday. Baptism, Holy Communion, and catechism were with the Roman Catholic Church. I was not invested in Church as a child. What I liked most were the clothes; my suits and coats, and my hat box with pretty choices. It would be a very long time before the significance of an upbringing involving church would have a major impact. Its vital importance would later be abundantly clear and literally save me from any harmful actions I might take in my despair.

My father did not allow me to go anywhere alone except the library. By the time I was ten, I was meeting with one of the librarians regularly. I would follow her around the library, and she would pile books she recommended high into my arms. I also eventually reviewed books for the library newsletter. I became a great reader, devouring books like *A Tree Grows in Brooklyn* before it was even appropriate. I also developed as a writer since I dreamed of being in a league with my favourites like Margaret Atwood, Leonard Cohen, and Margaret Laurence.

I blame my father for the most difficult aspects of my childhood, but it was also my super-sensitivity to things and his dramatic focus on the most serious matters. On sunny, breezy, relaxed summer days, he would haul my brother and me and our friends into the living room from the front porch to watch *Mutual of Omaha's Wild Kingdom* in order "to teach you kids something."

My mother may have been the positive one; however, it was negative Dad who listened to every story of hardship at the front door and always had a plan to help. Sometimes, Mom would get fed up and challenge him with, "Roman, are we heating the whole neighbourhood now?" He would walk toward Mom with the person now in the foyer. "Come on, Hon," he would coax, then in a barely audible whisper, "the poor guy . . ." Mother always relented.

Valerie lived across the street and shared my propensity to negativity. Barbara lived down the street, and we shared fathers who could be harsh. Who to better understand your traumas than girlfriends with their own? Valerie's mom remembered me as maturing early. "At sixteen, I would have trusted you with absolutely anything," she remarked.

One example is a New Year's Eve party that Valerie threw, inviting people without a lot of thought. The result was, some decided they were staying the night and had not been asked to do so. I called Valerie into the kitchen and said I could resolve the crisis with her permission. She gave it. The most practical thing I could imagine was to give them their coats! I knew it was rude, but then so were they. "Does anyone wish to claim this coat?" I asked. "Nice coat—black and grey." They got the idea quickly and were furious. Someone broke the staircase window on the way out. I had a new name: Mother. "Yes, we'll go because Mother says so. Bye, Mother, you b——."

Someone once asked, "Why do you think you have bipolar?"

I said, "I come by it honestly. My father seemed a bit depressed, and my mother, manic." I grew up in a very black-and-white world.

I knew early that there were clearly two sides to every single argument or situation. In addition, it created within me a certain open-mindedness.

Many years later, my friend Stan would tell me his daughter was jumping out of planes, skydiving. "I'm so proud of her!" he exclaimed. I tried to hide my sense of shock and repulsion because I was imagining *my* father's response. It would have been: "What the hell are you doing *that* for? Have you become completely crazy? Stop it now!"

I attended two different high schools and spent time in the detention room of the public one for talking too much. I would occupy myself by writing poetry:

Here we sit, row on row,
like in a garden where potatoes grow.
No talking is allowed, privileges are few,
I just sit and behave as the teachers tell us to.
We're the future of tomorrow and I ask,
"What about today?"
And I'm told to raise my hand
when I have something worthwhile to say.

(Cheryl Yarek, 1971)

It was parent-teacher night, and my mother was asked to attend. They told her I talked too much. "Well," she responded, "move her. Seat her somewhere else."

"Mrs. Yarek," my English teacher explained, "she has sat in every seat in this room, and she talks to everyone. There are students who have *never said a word*, but they speak to Cheryl!"

As I grew, the views of my conservative father and myself often clashed. He started to refer to me in my teens as, "My daughter, the hippie social worker with her far-out ideas." Despite our conflicts, I never doubted that my family loved me. Years later, I realized I was essentially searching my whole life for two things: an exciting career and a compassionate guy.

I went to the school guidance office with a question: "How old do I have to be to leave home and my father can't bring me back?" I was told I needed, in this case, to be sixteen years old. (I was fourteen-years old at the time.) I found that the next two years were the easiest of my childhood because I was so close now to independence. I did leave at sixteen, with a note on the table and carrying eleven Loblaws shopping bags on the subway. I felt convinced I would find the world less dictating than my father.

My girlfriends, Beth and Valerie, and I took up residence at Yonge Street and Eglinton Avenue in Toronto on a street named Broadway. We were always broke, rolling pennies for bread at the corner store. We ate interesting meals that Valerie's boyfriend occasionally cooked like veggies in a sauce with wieners. Leo's creations were creative and delicious. My positive regard for him changed, however, when he decided he wanted a threesome.

He kept pressuring me, asking why not. "'Cause I don't want to," came my reply. "That's why!" (Later, I was forced to move back to my parents' place as a temporary measure.)

My parents were clearly the opposite of each other. My father was the parent who exercised discipline and who taught it. My mother was never the harsh one. She was the understanding, supportive one with timely philosophies and thoughtful gifts. For my eighteenth birthday, I chose to fly to New York City. My mom gave me my birthday card ahead of time and clearly marked, "Only open in the air!" Inside were greetings for my special day as well as ample American dollars for shopping in the city.

My father was diagnosed with cancer and saw all the happenings in the neighbourhood from his bed beside the picture window in the living room, including the change of seasons. My mother insisted his hospital bed not be confined to a bedroom. I would stop by to enjoy long and interesting conversations with him. One time, he closed his eyes as I continued my story. In explanation, he remarked, "Honey, I'm listening to everything you're saying. I just have my eyes closed. I *love* to hear your voice." I treasured visits with my dad because he said the most beautiful things to me.

Mario, a neighbour, one day crossed the street to chat. "Your father is so proud of you," Mario relayed. I stopped and pointed toward the picture window. "Are you sure? Do you mean the man in *this house?*" I knew my dad loved, me but I didn't feel he was necessarily proud of me. Soon after, my dad told me himself, "I'm so proud of you. I know we never agreed, but I am so proud of you and what you have done with your life." These words completely and immediately resolved the years and years of conflict between us. My father's funeral took place on my 45th birthday. His enormous presence during some of the worst challenges of my life remained; the consolation.

One Mother's Day letter to my Mom read:

> You are an incredible mom. You have the phenomenal ability to teach by example. You not only support the dreams of your children; you are their central cheerleader. Many parents can help focus their kids in the area of rationality but extremely few start them off with Dreaming 101 as well. You are my mother, and I love you, but you are also one of my absolutely favourite people in the world. I meet few people as interesting as you. You are also exceedingly compassionate when it comes to the suffering and sorrow of others. More than that even, it motivates you to help through prayer, astrology, meditation, health teaching, and reading. You have never stopped evolving and growing. You have the special ability to empower others to feel better. This is because you win the award for Most Positive Person. Your confidence guides and directs us all. You also win the award for Fastest Smart Thinker. This makes you indispensable in many situations, especially emergencies. You even save lives. I am proud that you are my mother. Who wouldn't be? A superb conversationalist, you are also able to negotiate—seeing the other side. As my mother, you have never tried to rule me, but rather, given me the freedom to make my own choices and create my own path. You have supported and encouraged personal independence. I want to thank you especially for this, because it has brought me the greatest happiness.

Ryerson Followed by the Media

"I hired you because you exuded confidence."
Network supervisor in the media in 1979

When I changed electives from math and science to English and history in high school, I became a top-notch student. My average went from the mid-sixties to 87 percent in grade 13! For a degree program, I chose Ryerson Polytechnical Institute, where as students we were treated with respect and tender-heartedness. One student crew was even permitted to roll a studio camera into the men's washroom! Why? The powers that be agreed it would contribute to establishing the solidness of the plot.

It was 1976. Fifteen hundred people applied that year to study Radio & TV Arts, and they accepted 130 individuals. (I was one of them.) I was interviewed by the chairman of the department, Bob Gardner. Towards the end of the interview, he asked what I would do if I wasn't accepted into the program. I said the first thing that came to mind: "I'll cry." He laughed. Then I added, "And I'll apply again next year."

Upon acceptance, my grandmother paid my tuition fees and for my books. She expected me to pay my own room and board since I chose not to live with my parents. The first year was exclusively radio, and I wasn't completely interested. Second year and third year were television and film, and I really enjoyed myself. Someone coined a term: *hard fun*. We would say, "OK, let's have some hard fun—work very, very hard and have lots and lots of fun!"

I would need to work part-time while going to Ryerson. I saw a sign posted on a drugstore on Yonge Street (behind Ryerson). I went several times, attempting to speak to the manager about the position. I could tell he was trying to get rid of me, so I was direct and asked why. He sighed. "You're a very nice girl, and this is not a nice place." Billy said I wouldn't be able to handle the clientele. (A mix of business people, tourists, prostitutes, drug dealers, and people living in poverty.) In the end, I negotiated with Billy by saying, "This is the perfect job for me—perfect hours, perfect location, and perfect pay. Let me work one full weekend. On Sunday night, we talk. You don't like my work, you fire me. I'll leave, no questions asked." Billy gave me this chance despite his misgivings. Turns out, I worked at the store for three years. When I left to work in the media, Billy shook my hand with the comment, "You were the one cashier I never wanted to hire, and you were the *best* cashier I ever had." Billy said he learned a lot from our relationship. (Me too!)

In the second year at Ryerson, I co-produced and played the lead actress in a video I wrote called *A Fan in Search of a Star*. It was autobiographical, about my youth as a fan of Sonny and Cher. (I met Sonny several times and Cher once.) Our production won the Ryerson Radio and Television Arts award for Best Drama in 1979.

Martin, a friend from Ryerson, once connected with me at my parents place by phone. "Not very nice of you," he admonished.

"I don't understand," I replied. "What isn't nice of me?"

"Well," he said, "to be having a party and not inviting me!"

"Martin," I replied, "there is no party. That's my parents having *a conversation* in the background!"

My new job in the media was with the national newsroom at the network. There were issues. After one year, I approached Human Resources to address a concern: my supervisor's inappropriate advances. Their reply? They told me I was "too honest." I had always believed that there was only honest, and its opposite was dishonest. At twenty-two years of age, I was now asked to form the conclusion that honesty came in grades, like eggs. Perhaps there was "almost honest," "close to honest," and even "near honest." I was dealing with sexual harassment although officially the term had not yet been invented (1979–1982).

The next thing that happened was my supervisor showed up intoxicated on the overnight shift to propose marriage. He offered me "any living situation you wish for, just name it." I knew he was already married and had two young sons. When I mentioned this, he became very emotional and swore he would not only divorce his wife but make certain we gained "custody of the boys." I remember thinking: *Here is another person wanting to run my life, finding ways to annoy and disempower me.*

I would love to say all my thoughts on the matter were sound and clear, but that was not actually the case. The boundaries were blurred and fuzzy, and I was baffled and confused. Part of my confusion rested with the fact that I was ambitious and held one of the lowest positions on what we termed "the totem pole." He was my supervisor, and I had counted on him to help direct my course at work. It became obvious that his ambitions were for himself, not me. I wanted to leave the department (by applying for other positions), but he blocked the way each time very effectively. After all, he had the power to do so.

Into this continuing battle came another angle. Roy, who was the union representative, decided I was favoured by management, and he did not like it. He became very inquisitive and wanted to know how I became employed at the network. I said I was presently a student at Ryerson's Radio and TV Arts Program and I had worked part-time at a local drugstore before joining the network. With this, he ranted in the newsroom for days about how "you can work in a drugstore now and then get a job here!"

At the end of the year, I was called me into the management office to ask if I wanted full-time employment. "I'm not sure," I replied (my too-honest self).

"Well, you had better decide," she remarked. "There are at least one hundred people who want your job."

"Fine," I replied, "I'll take it."

Looking back, I had known from my first hour at the network that I did not belong there. The organization had a great reputation in the province, even the country; however, I began to feel embarrassed that I worked there, more aware than most of what went on behind the scenes.

At the network, I was referred to as "Mother Hen with her chicks" by the senior assignment editor. He said I did a good job looking after and supporting seven copy clerks. Naturally, their issues became my concern. One clerk was petrified of one of the writers because he was emotionally unstable. Sometimes, when angry, he slammed his desk drawer open and shut while cursing against the network. In the meantime, my supervisor called me to his office. He was firing the clerk who was intimidated by this writer! I explained that she was afraid of the writer for good reason. Wallace said this was unacceptable. I said I thought the *writer's* behaviour was "unacceptable," and I defended Cindy. Eventually, Wallace changed his mind about her firing. Back in the newsroom, Cindy cornered me. She sensed things were up. She was feeling extremely insecure. "Please just do your job," I cautioned. "Everything is OK." (I never disclosed anything to her about my meeting with Wallace.)

My feelings about my career in the media were very different from the feelings I had for Ryerson; I loved Ryerson and hated the media. In the end, I resigned. My supervisor's response? "I'm not accepting your letter!" he remarked. I just shook my head and left the building.

I suppose a lot of it was about growing up and realizing that reality can be very different from the world we might imagine. Funny enough, during my toughest days in the media, my standard line was, "Just ignore me. I'm only here to gather information for the book I'll write one day."

I mention my relationship with Jack here, and lastly, for a reason. It was a huge factor in my becoming depressed, psychotic, and ill. I met him at school and worked with him on a television production, which was an opportunity offered to us students. Later, when I started work at the network, I discovered he also worked there. I knew him for many years and was deluded enough to believe we might manage a future together. I was quite wrong.

The most harmful thing I learned from Jack was this: he introduced me to marijuana. We often got high together. (And I learned the hard way that drugs complicated every issue for me and marijuana was not a coping strategy or device—despite my imaginings at the time.) One evening, Jack told me that he had a plan in mind if he didn't succeed in his career. It went like this: "I'll kill myself and videotape it so I make the cover of the *Toronto Star*." Myself, I wasn't certain at the time, whether to call a distress line or emergency or just make like he had said, "The night is very dark tonight, dear," and leave rather quickly. I chose to leave rather quickly.

Having already left my job and the network, I was busy continuing my learning about the notion that you cannot win all battles, and it seemed nor are you meant to. In those days, however, I was not very eloquent, centred, or stable. If my dreams were a building, it felt like the foundation had given way and all the stories had collapsed and crumbled in a heap. It was also like an affront—akin to a slap in the face. I have to tell you, I wasn't coping well with my choice to leave the network, perhaps because it did not feel like a choice. At the same time, Jack threw a party and used the opportunity to introduce everyone to his fiancée. I did not expect this. In the end, I lost my footing. My psychosis began in their presence, and my awkwardness and coming undone, they found incredibly funny. It seemed now, everywhere I turned, someone else was laughing at me. The combination of losses—career, financial, friendship, and romantic—almost completely destroyed me.

It was at this juncture that I learned the most expensive lesson I was ever taught, and it arrived in an envelope I never expected to be handed: THE WORLD CAN DESTROY YOU.

Last Poem to Jack: "Through Glass"

I sit and watch as twenty minutes' worth of people pass
before I understand I have no reason to be waiting,
before I understand we agreed you would not return.
Too soon, I heard your retreat, like soldiers on the street.
I saw your wandering over half-filled coffee cups.
I saw your shoulder fashioning, an exact escape.
There were times I brought you faces,
collected from other rooms, spaces you had not
touched with your romance.

Now, I would like to be happy for you
but optimism is for those who believe in heaven
and I am so uncertain it holds a promise,
more perfect than your eyes.
My forgiveness is a sculpture.
It followed the blueprint of your closed eyes.
I once knew how they fell into
the exact nature of the universe.
Constantly now, I sit in this chair,
listening to my head pace.
Other people concern me because
I hear them through glass.
I listen back, calm with no answer.

(Cheryl Yarek, 1984)

The Horror of Psychosis

"I did not come and pluck you out of hell. You got out
of hell because you wanted to get out of hell."

My psychiatrist, 1984–2011

I was never ever, ever so lost. There seemed nowhere to turn, and my response was drastic—more street drugs. My search and my ambition were for one thing—to disappear without taking my life. Each time I used marijuana, the reality I returned to was more and more and more bleak. The last straw? Now, I was exhibiting symptoms of mental illness.

I felt forlorn and hopeless. I looked mentally ill and got stares on the buses and streets. The more some chose to laugh or gawk, the more I felt worthy of the abuse.

One day I took the subway then waited at Dundas West for a streetcar. A woman my age approached me. "Are you Cheryl Yarek?" she asked. Now, I was completely bewildered by this but said, "Yes." She told me she could not believe her good fortune to run into me. Ironically, I was convinced that no one on the planet cared if I lived or died. She said her name was Christine and she went to grade school with me. She said, back then, she was new to the country, the school, and barely spoke the language. "YOU," she proclaimed, "were wonderful to me. You tucked me under your arm and looked out for and protected me. You never judged. I always wanted to thank you and now here you are!" (I was certain I was far more amazed by the timing than Christine could ever be.) The encounter had a huge impact on me. It was as though God sent me an angel, one who held a bright and positive part of my history in her very hands. But I would continue to ponder the question: "Who am I?"

The despair returned and continued. I was home alone. The year was 1984. Suddenly, I heard some knocking coming from the basement. I was more afraid of what I could imagine than searching out the answer to this scary situation. The noise was coming from the fruit cellar room. I opened the door, and three things jumped out at me. I saw a large white Bible, an axe, and a plaque of the Virgin Mary. The items were positioned one beside the other, along a wooden shelf. I panicked and decided to call the police.

An officer arrived shortly. He checked the basement including the fruit cellar then toured the entire house, eventually saying he felt I was safe; there was nothing out of the ordinary. As he climbed the stairs to the front door, some photographs of me at my high school graduation caught his eye. "Is that you?" he asked, pointing.

"Yes," I replied.

"You must have been a real scholar," he remarked.

Somehow, I could not help adding in my own mind and to myself: *Before you lost your mind!*

When the officer left (I had perspective now), I returned to the fruit cellar room and decided to put things in their place. First, I took the axe and placed it in the garage. Then I closed the Bible and returned it to the library. Lastly, I hung the picture of the Virgin Mary above my bed. (Every time I have relocated, I have placed her above my bed, and she is still there thirty-three years later.)

I was often imagining how to safeguard myself. One day, I realized there would be safety and comfort in a blessing, so I took the King streetcar down Roncesvalles Avenue and got off at St. Casimir's. I went to the door of the parish, where the priests live and knocked. When a priest answered the door, I said, "Father, I am very afraid. Could you please just bless me?" And he did "in the name of the Father and the Son and the Holy Spirit." As I left, my mood lifted. I felt some level of protection.

Whenever I went out into the community, I was ridiculed, insulted, and openly laughed at—mostly by teenagers. Some people looked at me and made the sign of the cross. Sometimes my eyes did not focus and I couldn't control my thoughts. When thoughts came to me, they were like surprises. I stayed in the house because venturing out meant walking through a war zone. In my mind, the Third World War was being fought on the streets of Toronto between the Russians and North Americans.

A psychosis means you have lost touch with reality. It does not necessarily mean you are harmful. My psychosis began with nightmares and eventually the nightmares expanded to include what I named "daymares." I lay awake at night and hallucinated all day. I saw dead bodies piled along the sidewalks. I smelled blood and saw my mother as a Russian commander holding me captive. At the time, my mother worked as a supervisor at a shop at Pearson Airport. Not only did she snap at me regularly because she found me difficult to deal with, but she also wore a bright-red uniform to work. She hung this uniform on a picture nail in the living room so she would be able to locate it each morning. The red uniform could be seen through the sliding glass door in the kitchen, and I believed/imagined it was a signal to the Russian army.

I saw my father as an Italian architect assigned to work as my bodyguard. Although my father was neither Italian nor an architect, he was extremely interested in buildings. He often invited me for walks, and as we strolled, he would comment on and analyse the structure of the houses. I decided he was my bodyguard after a walk to the variety store one evening. As we made our way there, my thoughts told me I would be shot dead that evening. Even the Christmas lights on houses seemed to spark and emit tiny bullets aimed at me. Finally, I stood in one spot, frozen, and told my father how scared I was. He took it in stride and made this reply, "I've never told you this before, but my jacket, it's bulletproof (an untruth). If anyone comes near you, I'll block the shot." His reputation was for honesty, and this and his manner secured me.

I did have a greater fear than the war—I was scared of myself and what I might do, because according to the media, people mentally ill commit brutal crimes. Don't they? Meanwhile, the thought of hurting someone never occurred to me. The notion that someone might harm *me* was ongoing. After all, I hated myself and felt I deserved punishment as though feeling the way I did was not punishment enough.

There is nothing more frightening than an episode of psychotic depression. Even horror movies end. An episode of psychotic depression, untreated, can go on for years. My depression reached an extreme (psychosis) because it went on so long without any treatment. Any individual depressed for more than two weeks should seek medical attention. (Please note: statistically speaking, incidents of violence are no higher among those with psychiatric disabilities than the general population.)

Due to the many myths surrounding mental illness, I was terrified of myself and committing possible violence, so I prayed all the time. One prayer I repeated was, "Please, God, if I decide to hurt someone, please intervene and take my life immediately." I understood that I would not be able to live with the fact that I had seriously hurt someone or worse.

Only one person accepted me as I was—my father. He spent each morning and evening talking with me. If I did anything my mother found unacceptable, my father would rush to my defence. Once, I curled up on the living room carpet and began to make swirling motions with my fingers along the rug. This upset my mother, who raised her voice and announced that as soon as she could afford it, she was sending me straight to a psychiatrist. (My family was unaware that psychiatrists, being medical doctors, were covered by Ontario's healthcare plan.) My father calmed my mother down, saying, "If it makes her feel better, let her do it. She's not hurting anyone."

My brother had dressed for Halloween that year as a priest. He had the black robe hanging in his room afterwards. One night, I was standing outside his door which he opened to come into the hall. I scared him badly, and he leapt several feet into the air. After this, I overheard him tell my mother that he was terrified of me and what I might do. I figured then and there that possibly there was no hope for me—not if I was scaring a priest!

One evening, I was watching TV. There was a musical special, and David Bowie was a guest singing "China Girl." I remember thinking he looked very angelic. The next sensation I felt was that of clamps being applied to my head, breasts, stomach, and on down to my feet. Screws were then being inserted into the clamps, and everything was being tightened. I ran to the kitchen and shouted at my parents, "Please take me to a hospital! I can't take it anymore!" My father wanted to take me to Queen Street Mental Health Centre, but my mother won by arguing that "every general hospital has a psychiatric unit." The trip to the hospital seemed to take forever. I was certain I would die, never finding relief. Once there, I was escorted by staff to a wheelchair. I no longer possessed the energy to face the world—standing.

A nurse asked if I wanted my parents to accompany me in the examining room. "No!" I shouted. "They're not my parents! They're the Russian commander and the Italian architect! They're posing as my parents! My parents are dead."

I met Dr. Marie Philips on November 23, 1984, in the emergency department of Mountridge General Hospital in Toronto. I was first in a room where six hospital staff came and went. (I counted them.) Each asked why I was at the hospital. I replied, "It's because of the war."

"What war?" they asked.

"The Third World War," I replied.

This sent each quickly out of the room. Eventually, a woman carrying a notepad and pen entered. She was the only staff who sat down. The word *shrink* was like a shout in my head. "I hear you're not feeling very well." she remarked.

"No," I replied, "not since the war."

"And when did the war start?" she asked.

I was so overcome by her reasonableness and common sense, I felt like crying. I remember thinking, *She is the only truly normal human being I have spoken to in years.* She was the only person who permitted me to fully express my distress. People normally listened to one of two statements, then dismissed my views while verbally patting me on the head like a child. *This*, however, felt so freeing!

The positive feelings did not last, though. Dr. Philips was not going to hospitalize me—no beds. She called in my parents and told them I had psychotic depression. She described it as a depression that has gone on so long, the person is now out of touch with reality. The plan was that she would prescribe medication, and my mother would bring me to her office. Now? I hated Dr. Philips. If she had no hospital bed for me, she was no better than the rest—someone else who just now betrayed me. I could not possibly keep it together forever! I felt acute despair and pain.

My mother and I went to Dr. Philips's office as expected, but I refused to speak. Dr. Philips and my mother conversed as I stared out the window. I believed Dr. Philips was another betrayer, no different. My mother began to describe my activities the previous day. "She was covered in mud," she relayed. "She said she was digging in the front yard to uncover the bodies of her family." My mother was very disturbed, aghast. Dr. Philips looked at my mother, then at me, then at the sky outside her window. Finally, she remarked, "Mrs. Yarek, we all do a little bit of digging every now and then." Wow. I now loved Dr. Philips. I was never so impressed with anyone. When we arrived home, my father asked cheerfully, "How did it go with Dr. Philips?"

My mother snapped back, "Dr. Philips needs treatment herself!"

Dr. Philips had recommended "Daycare" at the hospital for me. When I heard her say this to my mother, I panicked and remarked, "But I'm too crazy to take care of other people's babies!" Both women burst into laughter. I was assured that the day care was for me. I was going to be taken care of. *That* sounded very pleasant.

Eventually, the medication seemed to be working. I began to feel better about myself. I rode the buses a lot—sometimes all day long. I started to view the critical comments of my fellow passengers as potentially helpful. I would use the feedback to my advantage, if I could. I tried to correct my behaviour as much as I could to conform. *My reasoning was this: Society had torn me apart. It seemed fitting that society might also have the power to put me back together.*

One day, with the best of intensions, I set out for day care. My father wrote the directions on a piece of paper, and I took the appropriate buses. When I got off in front of the hospital, though, my eyes zeroed in on the huge *H* at the top of the building. Well! To me, the *H* clearly stood for "hell," and undoubtedly, the plan was to cremate me. In my mind, I was focused on what I had heard happened in the Holocaust, and I wasn't going to go willingly into any oven! I grabbed the next bus, going anywhere as long as it was away from hell. Several hours later, I returned home. My father had received a call from the hospital, saying I had not arrived. He told me a spot had been "reserved" for me and I would miss this "opportunity" if I didn't go straight there the next day. He told me Susan Miller had called. I agreed to follow through the next day. Meanwhile, I went to my room to think. I sat on the edge of the bed and tried to decipher this latest puzzle piece.

For me, everything had a secret code, and if I could only continue to unlock the reoccurring mysteries, I would be spared from death. I knew the Russians wanted me dead. "Susan," I mused to myself, "Susan Miller." Oh my god! "Mill-her! Put her through the mill!" I decided then and there I would definitely *not* go to hospital tomorrow. I would ride the buses instead and work on improving my behaviour. I would never recover if I *let* them cremate me. "Susan," I said aloud. "Mill yourself!"

My father discovered despite my attempt to cover it up that I did not go to hospital the following day. I had not wanted him to know that I knew what the Russians were up to. After all, he was married to a Russian commander no less! It was now arranged that my mother would drive me to the hospital. I went without argument. I even tried to envision the positive side of cremation. For instance, perhaps I was too far gone to benefit from conventional treatment. Perhaps cremation would permit me to be born again, completely sane this time. My mother dropped me off at the hospital doors. I walked into the building and tried to remember the name of the department I was supposed to go to, but I couldn't remember. I knew it was day something. Suddenly, I read a sign that said "Day Surgery." That must be where I needed to go. I then imagined that my panic might be misplaced. It could be that I was going to be "taken care of" in a good way—as Dr. Philips had indicated. I reached the entrance to day surgery and paused. My hopes were instantly dashed. What I first saw were several people lying on beds. My heart began to thump. Were they being prepared for cremation? A nurse turned and made her way toward me. My gaze was now transfixed. She was carrying a clear plastic bag with a hairbrush, socks, shoes, and a wallet. I tore out of the hospital and caught a bus home.

Next, my brother was instructed to take me to hospital by bus. I went willingly because, in my mind, a priest was the appropriate escort to damnation. One day, while on day care, I collapsed. My legs which were often full of pins and needles gave out from under me. I fell in front of reception and was admitted to hospital immediately. I had not slept for several days and was in a state of constant terror. I was given medication and went to sleep. As I closed my eyes, I was certain I would never wake again.

When I awoke, I was completely shocked, and my eyes watered. I sat up and felt the bed around me, realizing that I was not dreaming. I then touched my own hands and arms. Into my mind came the following words: "Life is a gift. Life is a gift from God." I was overwhelmed with emotion and cried, then prayed, "God, I know I will recover. You seem to be sending me *that* message. And when I do recover, I want to make You a promise. I will dedicate the rest of my life to helping others in mental distress. I'll start with volunteer work as soon as I'm able to." (Then more cheerfully I said, "I'm going to have a career in mental health someday!") *One of my goals became to create awareness around mental illness stereotypes because I believe stigma will always exist until some of those who have faced issues like psychosis, suicide, and drug addiction have the courage to make their discoveries, common knowledge.*

What hurt the most about my psychosis was being laughed at by people when it was abundantly clear I had already fallen. I swore I would never ever, ever forget the humiliation. My greatest pet peeve became the mocking of suffering. It infuriates me to this day. One of my nurses at the hospital said to me, "It took a long time for us to know how to help you. You kept saying you were 'buried.' Now we realize you *were* buried and our job was actually to unearth Cheryl!"

My mother bought me a poster. The photograph was of a wooded area in winter with lots of snow and the sun shining in a brilliant way through the trees. The accompanying Albert Camus quote read: "In the midst of winter, I finally learned there was within me, an invincible summer."

One day, I was on my way to day care. I was standing at the bus stop. I was still very ill but now had a psychiatrist, day treatment program, and an illness with a name. I felt filled with gratitude. I made certain no one was watching me at the bus stop, and I bowed my head and prayed out loud these words: "Thank you, God. Thanks, God. Thank you so much, God. Thank you, Holy Father. Thanks." The bus shelter was near a traffic light and suddenly a shuttle bus pulled up to the light. Written on a diagonal on the side of the bus in huge letters were the words, "You're welcome."

My family made their displeasures and their solutions clearly known at this time. They could not get over the fact that I had changed my name from Cheryl to Roma. (Roma is my middle name.) I truly could not relate to their dismay. I snapped at my mother, "For God's sake, I'm not calling myself Betty! Roma *is* my name!" My mother decided to start a clothing business and have me work there to manage the store. As is customary in my family during any perceived crisis, I was not consulted. Perhaps they believed I was too crazy to appreciate the sheer brilliance of the idea. I was only paid fifty dollars weekly for my efforts. This was to ensure that (1) I did not buy any drugs and (2) I did not shack up with a current boyfriend. In fact, in a continuing attempt to end romance between myself and this boyfriend, my brother arrived at a venue to confront him. Darrell, however, had never seen the likes of community artists, and some of the artwork was offensive, very contrary to our Roman Catholic upbringing. My brother ended up leaving—very much more than shocked.

The success of my mother's business was tied to my moods. When manic, I took in a lot of money; when depressed, I didn't. I loved to make tea for my favourite customers, and this did not have to do with how much they spent but with my fondness for them as people. The store was across the street from the Queen Street Mental Health Centre's Outreach Program: Archway. My mom permitted me to close the business and attend workshops there occasionally. And there were some items I was permitted to give away if someone needed them—usually underwear and/or socks. One woman was so grateful, she repeated many times, "No one has ever done anything for me!" There was one man who stopped by for tea with his German shepherd. He said the dog was a guard dog and for hire to watch over the store at night. I explained that this wasn't a necessity since money was never left on the premises. Fortunately, my mother had no issues about who drank tea at the store, and she endorsed the occasional giveaways to those in need.

When my recovery from the psychotic depression was almost complete, I would sit with a psychologist at the hospital, and he would ask if I remembered anything about my psychosis. "Yes," I replied, "I remember *everything*." (I learned this type of remembering is quite uncommon in individuals experiencing a psychosis.) I explained that when I walked down the street, I smelled blood and saw dead bodies piled along the sidewalks.

"You were certain they were there?" he asked.

"No," I replied, "I think they were superimposed like one picture on top of another."

"Why did you think that?" he enquired.

"Because I learned superimposition at Ryerson and because of the normal expressions of the other people I passed on the street. They looked like they weren't seeing dead bodies piled along the sidewalks."

The psychologist thought for a minute then said to me, "You are very intelligent."

"Or very lucky," I replied.

Bulletin from the Unemployed

I'm here alone with my head, waiting for
the people who work to come home.
I talk to the television, mostly I argue with it—
a slight touch of psychotic paranoia.
The media and people wearing sunglasses,
irrational fears?

(Cheryl Yarek, 1990)

Volunteer Work, Supportive Housing, and Freelancing

I commissioned my hospital notes. In 1985, while I
was an inpatient, a nurse wrote in my notes, "Cheryl
has the delusion she will work in mental health
someday." Well, here I am *living my delusion!*

Author

The first place I approached for a volunteer position was the
Clarke Institute of Psychiatry. I was very open about my disability since I saw it as an asset. The volunteer coordinator
told me there was no suitable position for me presently but they
would contact me in the future. To be honest, I didn't believe this.
I felt rejected and believed it was because I was too honest and said
too much. In fact, I was so disappointed, I walked from there to the
Queen Street Mental Health Centre. (Anyone who knows Toronto
will realize the considerable distance I travelled due to my upset!)

At the centre, I was introduced to Joyce, the volunteer coordinator. She interviewed me immediately in her office. I was still
speaking when she stood up, opened a drawer, removed a name tag
with volunteer at the top, and she wrote on the bottom, "Cheryl." It
was a huge battle not to burst into tears. After all, I had risen to the
level of "volunteer." Joyce readied me for a tour of the facilities and
partnered me with Rosie to serve tea—in real china cups—to the
patients on Sundays.

While at the centre (one year), the impossible happened; the
Clarke Institute called! They offered me both a training program and

a position helping patients find employment. They even gave me a temporary office. Dr. Brooke was in charge of the training program, and she was and is an amazing person. Her belief in my abilities was strong, and she thought I could pursue psychiatry. Dr. Philips dismissed the idea with the remark, "Too stressful."

My favourite volunteer position, though, was at a distress centre. I was there for two and a half years, and the role convinced me I wanted a career in mental health. The call I remember best was from an older woman who was home alone and depressed. She assured me she was going to execute a plan to end her life and "there is nothing you can do about it." Fortunately, she was wrong. I used the business line to call 911, who traced the call on the crisis line (I was engaged on two phones) and sent an emergency unit to her home. When the police reached her, they took the phone and said, "It's all right, Cheryl, we have it from here. Thanks for your work, and someone will call you." I started to cry but contained it. A female police officer called on the business line to debrief and counsel me. The amount of energy the call required was so stressful, I had a cigarette in the washroom of the non-smoking building. Being treated with such respect and caring by the police told me I needed to be proud of myself for what I had done as *they* clearly were.

For many years, I supported the hospital where I was a client with monthly donations. (This was an early promise to God.) I also later sat on the Accreditation, Research, and Crisis Prevention Committees there. I viewed my psychiatrist's office as a port for myself and my boat. I knew, in case of shipwreck, I would always be pulled to safety. I also supported Aid to Women for many, many years. It's an agency that provides monies, materials, and emotional support to women who are pregnant and often alone. It helps these individuals choose life-affirming options, bringing their babies to term.

I decided to start a tradition, and I chose Valentine's Day. For the next twelve years, I delivered a Valentine's Day cake to my client hospital, inpatient unit. I also provided coloured plates, serviettes, cutlery, and a tablecloth. On this day, when we celebrate love, I needed to remember where I have been. For many years, I utilized the bakery that was nearest the hospital. I didn't drive then, and staff at the bakery, when they learned of my gesture towards the patients, were so impressed, they drove me to the hospital with the cake each year for five years!

While receiving ODSP (Ontario Disability Support Program), I spent five years doing volunteer work in the community, and while volunteering at the distress centre, I realized I definitely wanted a career in mental health. I decided to return to school and applied to York University to study psychology. Sometime shortly after, I was accepted into the honours BA program with plans to one day go to graduate school.

Understand, however, I was still not fully well. In some ways, I was still impaired. For example, socially, I was petrified and rather hopeless, so when I attended my first class and there were five hundred people in the lecture hall, I felt like breaking into song and dancing. Now, I would be exactly what I wanted to be—a number. (I wouldn't be centred out.) My grades were posted like everyone else's on a wall in the lecture hall under my student number. I did not need to talk or interact with anyone, and I was in heaven. This went on for two years. In third year, things changed.

I had been advised to take a course in small group process. The minute I walked into small group process, I felt exposed. I didn't like it. We were in groups of seven, and there was nowhere to hide. I did not speak for three weeks, not a peep. Next, I was crying on the bus all the way home each week. Two people in the group were humoured by my evident distress. It felt horrendous to be laughed at on top of everything else and was a trigger back to my depressive psychosis episode. Also, the group setup (circle of seven) reminded me of group therapy without the understanding. I felt as though my entire future was now questionable. I might even fail this course and not receive my degree. I saw Dr. Philips, and she was not helpful.

"I predict you will get an A in this course," she remarked.

Oh my, I mused, *even my psychiatrist has lost her mind!*

I pondered on the issue for several days. Finally, I decided there was nothing left to do but put all my cards on the table. I would tell my full story, and it would be a huge disaster or a huge success. The biggest issue for me in group was that it was a flashback for me to therapy group in hospital. As I sat down in group that week, I remarked, "I have something to say." I had the entire attention of the group at that point because I had never spoken before. I then read from my papers as though making a speech. When I stopped speaking, the group was speechless, and my life there changed that afternoon. I made several connections and one close friend. And believe it or not, I did get an A in small group process as predicted by my intuitive psychiatrist!

I met Natalia at York University. She was in my "small group process" class. We shared an important friendship for several years. Later, she moved with her husband to Israel. Before departing and speaking like a true psychology major, she remarked, "I know you have bipolar, and I know people with bipolar sometimes kill themselves. Cheryl, don't you dare. If I ever hear you killed yourself, I will find your grave, and I swear, I will dig you up personally. Do you understand?"

"Yes, Natalia," I replied, "I understand." Listening to her heartfelt remarks, I was *both* laughing and crying.

In 1990, I applied for a job in mental health / supportive housing. (My mother saw it advertised in the *Toronto Star* newspaper.) I was interviewed by the director and the residential manager, and I found the interview quite reasonable. What I remember most though was their final question: "How do you feel about carrying a pager?" This made me think of Dr. Philips since she was the only person I had ever met who carried one. I felt like saying, "I would be honoured to carry the pager," but instead, I just said, "That wouldn't be a problem." Soon after speaking to my references, they told me that the position was mine. It was one of the happiest days of my life! It was my first full-time and paid position in mental health! It had taken me five years or perhaps it was thirty-three! (I was thirty-three years old.)

Not long after starting the position, I developed anxiety issues at work. I'm confident it was the result of an over-attentive supervisor. My partner and I decided I needed a counsellor specific to anxiety. I was referred to a psychologist who was also the chief of psychology at my client hospital. His rate in 1990 was 150 dollars per hour. I saw him for sixty minutes. He used hypnotism, but I was not able to relax around him sufficiently for him to hypnotise me. Louis, my partner, asked why. I was honest. "Intuitively, I just don't trust him," I remarked. After this failure, I took private lessons with my yoga instructor. She had me memorize a series of postures, and I was back to work in a couple of weeks. It seems the chief gained fame for behaviour both despicable and criminal. My mother showed me his picture, years later, on the cover of the *Toronto Star*. He was charged with sexually assaulting two female patients.

I was fired in 1995 by my supportive housing employer because I became ill and had problems handling the role. It was one of the worst days of my life. I loved the job and the clients and the field. Dr. Philips wanted to intervene, but I would not permit her to. My reasoning was that I didn't want to be rehired by an agency that had chosen to dismiss me. My answer? Street drugs, again. Upon hearing this, Dr. Philips was so disgusted, and her remarks so derogatory, I went home, smoked all the dope I had on hand, then never bought or used ever again.

The Human Rights Commission had deemed my case a wrongful dismissal, and I hired a lawyer. He was the most confused person I have ever dealt with. He made constant mistakes and blamed his secretary for each one of them. He wrote and mailed letters stating the complete opposite of what I had directed. Due to his incompetence, I telephoned and said I was refusing to pay my last outstanding bill. I insisted he cease and desist (words my father taught me). I was dropping the case against the agency.

In 1996, I applied to a government program: SEA (Self-Employment Assistance Program). Louis, my common-law husband, had the ingenious idea of my starting a freelance writing business in mental health. However, by the time the interview was arranged, I was again deteriorating mentally. I arrived at the interview with Peter, very, very manic. I mentioned a bunch of grandiose, ridiculous ideas despite the fact that I had submitted a very workable business plan. Peter looked uncomfortable and kept excusing himself to speak to someone behind a closed door at the end of the room. Eventually, he told me I was not at my best, and he could not accept me into the program. However, he welcomed me to apply the following year. His manner was so incredibly considerate and supremely kind I trusted him and his advice and did apply the following year. I was healthy, and now they accepted me!

My business consultant in the SEA Program was Mourad. His first meeting with me was to establish my path within the program. He said I needed to add something to the writing role. "You're very outgoing," he remarked. "What about adding public speaking?"

"Sure," I replied as I was willing to try something new. Mourad asked me what writing I would start with in my business. "I've written an article on psychiatric medication," I offered.

"And who will you try and market it to?" he asked.

"The *Toronto Star*," I replied.

He looked very surprised, remarking, "I don't think the *Toronto Star* is ready for you!" Still, no one was more delighted than Mourad when the *Toronto Star* bought my article and named it "Some of Us Need Our Meds." It was the *first* article I sold as a freelance writer.

In July 1997, I took the "Work on Track Program" at Seneca College. My counsellor was Debby, a caring, supportive person with a wish to help promote my writing and speaking in the community. Together, we arranged a volunteer placement at FAME (Family Association for Mental Health Everywhere). I loved the environment, a lot of very focused, dedicated, and strong women, beginning with Judy Wallace, the executive director. The staff—Judy, Maria, Alenka, and Liliana—were always battling for me. Liliana was my immediate supervisor, and in one test she gave, she scored me as "exceeding expectations" in seventeen out of seventeen areas of work responsibility. Alenka was my confidant. I loved to speak to her about everything and anything. She was acceptance personified. Maria heard about my desire to speak in public and approached Judy. The next thing I knew, there was a flyer with my name on it and the title I imagined for my first speech: "Recovery from Psychotic Depression." My speech was scheduled for Monday October 20, 1997, at 7:30 p.m. in Etobicoke at the FAME office. It was the very first time I spoke in public about my recovery.

My speech at FAME met with a ready reception, and I was asked to speak at all three locations, which I did. I also presented this particular talk to Reconnect Mental Health Services, Community Progress, and to medical students at the Clarke Institute, the following year.

My time without regular paid employment, however, was turning from months into years. I had tried everything but prayer. When I prayed, I heard God tell me to call the director of the supportive housing agency. She was the person who literally handed me my pink slip! God wanted me to converse with her? Oh my gracious, I thought, could God be wrong? I listened to God's direction, however, because my dad taught me you listen to God. He will help when no one else can. I called the agency and left a message. The director called me back the same afternoon (it was late in the week) and invited me to see her at her office on Monday at 9:00 a.m. I was agreeable.

When I sat down with the director on Monday, I was so distraught, confused, muddled, and a general-basket case, I asked her for a job! She looked more than mildly surprised. (Guess so!) "Cheryl," she explained, "right now, you are on the books suing us!" I mentioned about the lawyer, the dropped lawsuit, and my refusal to pay the final bill. "He must have left the case open to get even with me," I offered. The director was willing to negotiate, and she asked if I would write a letter saying I would not sue in the future. After being blacklisted for years and now sent by God Himself, it seemed a very reasonable request. The director remarked that she would ask my former supervisor to write a positive letter of reference for me. "You were a very good employee," she explained. The director also began writing a list of her personal contacts in the business—all of whom she welcomed me to approach for employment. (Most importantly, this director who fired me told me about a position she believed would best suit me—peer support worker on an ACT team. I pursued this avenue and eventually landed my dream job.)

I left the meeting with the director on a high. I did send her a thank-you note in the mail explaining that although "I had come to do major bridge repair, I certainly wasn't expecting YOU to arrive with your own lumber and nails!"

I began to apply to the ACT teams in Toronto and specifically for the peer support worker position. To assist me, I joined the Job Finding Club at Humber College. Once we had all been in the group for several weeks, we wrote index cards with compliments for one another. The thirteen other participants wrote the following:

1. Ability to stay calm in crisis situation.
2. You are a gift to all of us. I've enjoyed your excellent feedback and insight. We were truly fortunate to have you in this group.
3. You manage to keep all situations light and make others feel OK to open up because of your honesty and ease.
4. If I could know myself one-quarter as well as you know yourself, I would be so lucky. Love your writing and humour.
5. Great insight, honesty; you really know who you are and where you are going.
6. Very informative and great sense of humour. Well-spoken and honest.
7. Very articulate. Really listens when others speak and gives great feedback. Very knowledgeable in your field of work. Please help a lot of people as you will.
8. Full of energy and a smile. Always a listener with a few kind and helpful words when necessary. Your straightforward approach and ability to be articulate in an interesting way is always refreshing (and quite rewarding for us).
9. Very insightful, attentive, and creative. I appreciate your input in interview very much.
10. Great writer, creative, great sense of humour, great speaker, and honest.
11. Hi, Cheryl. You have come a long way with a lot of hope. Wish you well.
12. A warming personality and keep your hope up.
13. Cheryl, you are so great. Calming, warm, insightful, focused, awesome laugh and smile. Great communicator.

I remember thinking, "With this kind of feedback and help, how can I fail?" (And I didn't. I had three interviews for peer support work with three ACT teams.)

Advice

"You would feel much better," she said,
"if you didn't think so much."
"Aren't you being redundant?" I asked.
"Aren't you saying I would feel better if I
didn't think?"
"There you go again . . ." she said.

(Cheryl Yarek, 1995)

The ACT Team

"In terms of our expectations for you in your position,
you completely and fully surpassed all those."

Trillium Mental Health Manager, 2000

My introduction to ACTT (assertive community treatment team) didn't begin positively. In fact, one of the unhappiest moments of my life was being hired by an ACT team, then fired moments later when the manager asked, then understood, I didn't drive. It was probably the most brief and intense bipolar experience of my life! Eventually, I received a call from Nora about a position at Trillium Health Centre on their South Etobicoke ACT team. The conversation was predictable and pleasant until I asked for directions to the site. "You can take the QEW," Nora replied. I let Nora know I didn't drive, trying hard to help her cancel the interview. But instead, she remarked, "That's OK, everything is negotiable." To this day, my three favourite words in the English language combined are, "Everything is negotiable!"

Following the interview on November 8, 1999, I started my position at Trillium as peer support worker on the South Etobicoke ACT team. A year later, in 2000, my manager spoke to me in a private meeting about my role. I was surpassing their expectations. I could not have been happier! There was a plan, she divulged, to promote me to case manager. She wanted to know if I thought it might be a driving position or would I continue to use public transit? I was in my forties and petrified to drive. In the end, to decide, I asked myself, "If you won't face your fears, can you honestly ask your clients to face theirs?" I chose to drive and take extensive lessons. One of my problems was that I was a smoker at the time and considering the purchase of a car. It became clear that I could not afford to smoke and drive, so I tried to reason it through. The car clearly represented my future, and smoking began to materialize as part of my past. Did I want all this bad enough to conquer a twenty-eight-year addiction? Cigarettes were my best friend. They saw me through every trial. Every reaction to good or bad involved a cigarette. What would I fill the emptiness with?

If my parents could ever have wished one single thing for me, it was that I might quit smoking. (In fact, my dad later said it was the greatest joy he experienced during the course of his illness—seeing me as a committed non-smoker.) My mother wanted to help, so she arranged an expensive session with a healer to get me started. It was a phenomenal beginning. The healer took a history the way any professional would. I was asked to recall what I did before I smoked. This was very revealing. I ice-skated, I biked, I danced, I walked, I roller-skated, I sledded, and I was a synchronized swimmer and long-distance runner. It became clear that I replaced positives with a negative—smoking. Activity had been stressed in my family. The healer explained the effect of physical movement on the brain and then advised me to return to my former level of exercise. I knew this was impossible because I could barely breathe now whenever I exerted myself.

I chose a driving school I believed in. I knew I would pay more, but they had a solid reputation. I imagined I might be using these skills indefinitely in my personal and professional life. Eventually, I would even be expected to transport clients. I had three fantastic instructors. Steve was my first instructor. He was amazing—very, very tolerant with me. The first two lessons I took with him, I refused to budge from the passenger seat.

"How do you expect to learn?" he asked, astonished.

"By watching you pilot the car," I replied.

In the meantime, I spoke to my cousin Carolyn and explained the passenger's seat. "Oh," she remarked, "that doesn't sound very good." She took it upon herself to telephone Uncle Pete and negotiate help for me.

For six months, I took the train to Brantford every weekend. (It was a city with a smaller population and less traffic.) In Brantford, I met with Uncle Pete. He would meet me at the train station with his pickup truck, and I would take over the driving. I was still smoking since driving made me anxious. "Cherie," he would say, "it's time to put out the cigarette and get behind the wheel."

That was my cue—the one that petrified me but that I listened to nonetheless. One of my first mistakes was to drive right up on the curb at the drive-through at Tim Hortons.

"What are you doing here?" Uncle Pete asked.

"I don't know," I replied, flabbergasted myself.

I was driving in Brantford for a few weeks when Steve dropped by from the driving school for my lesson. He stayed seated in the driver's seat, thinking I would head for the passenger's side. I went to the door of the driver's side. "Steve," I advised, "you'll have to get out."

"Why?" he asked, already familiar with our routine.

"I'm going to drive the car," I relayed.

"This car?" he asked.

"Yes," I explained, "I have been driving in Brantford, and now I'm ready to drive here." Steve was flabbergasted.

Steve had a very reassuring way about him. "Cheryl," he remarked, "I know you are afraid, even petrified to drive. However, I have always felt you were in control as you drove the car. I can guess what you are thinking and anticipate what you will do. I cannot say that about everyone. Some people look to the right then steer the car straight into oncoming traffic. In spite of your fears, you drive as though you are in control."

Sometime later, I asked about Steve of my third instructor. She remarked, "He's in charge of the *really* difficult cases now—the people who might *never* learn to drive." (I guessed—I imagine correctly—that I probably assisted Steve to formulate his specialty!)

Joseph Grant was the clinical leader at the agency that hired then, moments later, fired me because I didn't have a driver's license. When he learned I was at Trillium, working toward a license, he involved himself. Each and every time I did a driving exam ("pass or fail"—his words), he took me for an elegant lunch. A few years later, I learned his wife worked for Trillium. I ran into her at a mental health celebration. She walked up to me and said, "Hi, Cheryl, my husband thinks the world of you." I smiled and replied, "And your husband has a very secure wife!" We laughed a lot and hugged.

I won a President's Gold Leaf Award 2001 at Trillium Health Centre for writing the best journal article, that year. It was a long way from being diagnosed with psychotic depression in 1984 and bipolar disorder in 1995. Years of therapy taught me that when you live enough to make a lot of mistakes, you learn more than average as well. I had rebuilt my life, including liking myself a whole lot more and establishing healthy relationships. I had been directed, guided, and inspired out of a psychological wilderness by mental health professionals, and I respected them *so much* I became one!

Dr. Ryan Forbes was our consulting psychiatrist on the ACT team for almost five years. He could not have tried harder to draw my views from me and secure and empower me. I adored him. In 2004, he left for a medical clinic in Etobicoke, Ontario. I was in charge of writing any speeches necessary for the team, so it was me who needed to formally address his upcoming departure. It was very, very difficult. My speech went as follows:

Dr. Forbes,

I almost didn't write this speech because I would have to face how much I'll miss you . . . how much we'll all miss you, and that is not a comfortable place to be. You have been our consulting psychiatrist from the very beginning of the team. You have shared some stressful times with us, and we have shared even more moments together in laughter. We could always count on your wit and keen sense of humour to bring relief and levity to any situation. In addition to your humour, we were all touched by your supreme kindness. You were kind and considerate to each and every client, and your gracious manner extended itself to each one of us. As a team, we always knew we could count on you to be there for us, and you were reliable to a fault, even calling more than once from the airport. You gave added meaning to the word *dependable*. From a clinical point of view, your observation skills are exceptional and the fact that the clients loved you speaks more volumes than I can ever write. So although I am sad, I am also happy. If that sounds like a bipolar statement, it certainly is! I am delighted to remember that I shared four and a half years on this team with you. What a superb blessing! Dr. Forbes, our warmest wishes to you in all your future endeavours. Stay well. Stay the extraordinary person you are!

Cheryl Yarek
On behalf of the ACT Team
March 29, 2004

In 2005, I attended the Mountridge General Hospital Advisory Council for Crisis Intervention. Dr. Philips and Joseph Grant also sat on the committee, and this pleased me. During the "sharing of information" part of the meeting, I said I would be speaking at the ACTT conference and remarked to Dr. Philips, "So if you feel someone is talking about you, they are!" Everyone laughed. Ellen, another committee member, said, "Cheryl had the accreditors in tears at the last accreditation." This was my first time hearing this. Ellen then asked, "What do you make of your phenomenal success?"

I smiled and replied, "Sometimes I am driving my car and asking myself, Do I really drive? Am I driving this car? Do I actually own this car?"

Everyone laughed. Another council member noted that she had never had the opportunity to hear me speak. Ellen resolved then and there to have me speak again to the "day treatment" clients. I was also asked to be Mountridge General Hospital's Consumer Designate for 2006, which I promptly agreed to. I left the meeting, feeling on top of the world.

On Thursday October 6, 2005, I presented at the ACTT conference in Toronto, Ontario. Arriving at the Delta East Hotel, I ran into Helen, a colleague working in Ottawa. I asked her which speaker she was seeing next. "You!" she replied. It was superb to share refreshments before presenting with a friendly and supportive person.

I walked into the room where I would be speaking and took my computer out of its case. I placed my handouts in two stacks on a front table. The room was arranged like a nightclub with four to five chairs per table. While waiting for AV, I spoke to Janine, Daniel, and Dwight, who hugged and kissed me. My room monitor was Paddy, and I liked her genuine nature immediately. We went over my introduction, and Paddy left to bring me a glass of water. AV arrived, had problems, but they were soon resolved. More and more people were pouring into the room. My watch said 3 p.m., but Paddy had 2:55 p.m. Paddy remarked, "I'd start, Cheryl. You have a good crowd."

"Let's begin," I agreed.

Paddy introduced me, after which I outlined the format for my session—twenty minutes' personal journey, fifteen minutes for my six concepts of recovery, and ten minutes for questions. I began my speech, and my left hand shook visibly for five minutes. I decided to just keep shaking since I could not control it. Later, the nervousness vanished. The first dramatic audience reaction was to the "You're welcome" bus story. They burst into laughter. When I added, "I swear this really happened," they laughed louder. The second dramatic reaction came in response to one inpatient nurse saying, "Cheryl has the delusion she will work in mental health someday." They *loved* this story, and applause followed.

Next, I walked to the podium to begin my recovery PowerPoint presentation. I mentioned the handouts, which included my "sweeping questions," calculated to clarify values and help with relationships. Suddenly, there was a long line-up for the handouts. The question period followed. Someone asked about my pro-psychiatry stance. I admitted that my concepts were based on my personal experience and might not suit everyone. I said, "My way is not the only way to recover, admittedly." The second question was baffling. She asked, "Have you ever been psychotic and on the pager?"

I asked her, "Do you mean the client is psychotic or I am psychotic?"

"You," she replied.

"No," I said.

The question period ended up being twenty minutes long, and two people from the audience introduced themselves—Dwight Byrd and Dr. Suzanne Legault. They spoke about how they knew me and why they admired me. I was very honoured. Many times during the question period, I would respond with "I've never heard of that!" or some other casual remark, and the audience would roar with laughter. Paddy appeared at my elbow with the whisper, "Three more questions." Then it was over. Paddy said a few words in closing, and the audience applauded.

Many people came forward with more questions. Afterwards, I said to the ACTT clinical leader, "I want that martini you promised me!" She and Dr. Legault broke out laughing. They felt this presentation topped one I had done in Hamilton because "the questions were much more difficult to answer." Both women felt I handled it all with class. I said bluntly in reply, "I am representing Trillium."

I saw Helen again before leaving the hotel. "You are an absolute natural at public speaking!" she exclaimed, adding, "I'm not bullsh——ing you." She said my pacing was exceptional, especially around the humorous parts. Helen said she left when the woman asked the question about the pager because "I was going to lose it, otherwise." Helen explained, "You know, you created such a comfortable atmosphere with your speech, even the *stupid* people were asking questions!"

Years earlier, my experience in meeting my psychiatrist left me thinking this:

> I give you my hands, I give you my voice.
> Please be gentle with me because I am human,
> and I have been beaten up for it.
> I bring you my mistakes which ask forgiveness.
> I give you the power, if you wish, to change
> the course of my life.

My colleagues on the ACT team sent me to meet a client. "But I don't work with her," I remarked. "Bring her medications to her," they instructed. I telephoned her, and we met at a specific time, street, and place—where she meets staff every week. I put down the passenger window to facilitate the delivery, and she leaned in the window, talking with me for about thirty minutes. She told me her story, in brief, and asked to work with me.

I had to follow protocol (get permission), and the team's response was a resounding yes! (In fact, this seemed their plan.) She and I had several meetings, after which I advised her, "You will go very far in your recovery because you have the super-honesty it takes." After our work together was complete and as we went our separate ways, I swear I had heard her say:

> I give you my hands, I give you my voice.
> Please be gentle with me because I am human,
> and I have been beaten up for it.
> I bring you my mistakes which ask forgiveness.
> I give you the power, if you wish, to change
> the course of my life.

One time at work, I mentioned that I did not have an answer to a problem at the table because I don't have children. One of the staff replied with a smile, "Actually, Cheryl, you have eighty!" Everyone laughed. (Our team served eighty clients.)

Sometimes, I have tried to elicit the expertise of the client. For example, I planned to make shortbread for the first time. I remembered one client saying she makes shortbread for Christmas each year. I telephoned her during work, because I found my recipe confusing. She clarified around the details of the recipe, adding some tips. One of her supportive comments was, "Don't worry, Cheryl, it's actually hard to screw up shortbread!"

In 2007, my employer made a decision to provide me with an accommodation in terms of on-call work. I would no longer have to carry the pager. My manager spoke to me soon after though about going to EAP for anger training. The issue was anger directed at my supervisor. I accepted the referral. I was dealing with many, many issues at work. (Dr. Philips once said, "If there had not been so many problems and concerns, you would have been bored and left years before." This was a very astute observation, and I would say that Dr. Philips perhaps knew me better than anyone else.) For many, many years, I was able to resolve any conflicts with colleagues through a discussion with them—never involving management. As the workload increased, as there were more and more long-term absences due to illness (leaving us perpetually short-staffed), I was less able to cope with the addition of conflict. One of the nurses, Rita, and I had issues. One day, I initiated an open discussion between us, and this was the beginning of better relations. I let her know that I thought our differences were caused by our strengths being very similar. Several days later, I followed up with a thank-you card and ten packages of sugarless gum tied together with colourful ribbons—left on her desk. (Gum chewing was a liking we shared.)

Rita reassured me about my anger: "You have this because everybody has something. You are a great girl. Don't forget it!" Now, my eyes were full of tears. Before sending me off, Rita hugged me, and I hugged her back. When it was suggested that she go to EAP, Rita resigned. Before leaving, she told me, "Cheryl, if you were to retire tomorrow, you would still have helped hundreds and hundreds of people. The clients more than love you—they worship and idolize you."

In 2008, my impatience with my supervisor and her harsh and confusing directives reached "unbearable." I decided to report her to the mental health manager and started to document our interactions. I then let my EAP counsellor know my plans, reading from the papers I had prepared. I met with Lenore, the manager, twice. I felt heard, valued, and very relieved. After our meeting, I sent her this email: "I really appreciate all the time you set aside for me and my concerns. Your approach not only helped me to solve my issues; I learned an incredible amount in the process. To have a manager to go to whom I feel comfortable with and who hears me and who provides adequate time for thinking and self-reflection is like being provided with a little piece of heaven at work. Thanks so much."

I also included remarks made by my EAP counsellor: "Trillium is a place where you feel very secure and safe." He said my sense of security in the workplace is what allowed me to learn to drive at age forty-three, quit smoking after twenty-eight years, and pursue EAP help. I added in my letter to the manager this remark: "I cannot say it any more effectively than Ken White (CEO), who when describing Trillium once remarked simply, 'Wow!'"

The decision to become a mental health professional while remaining a client at an alternate hospital has largely been a healing journey for me. It has permitted me to give up my worst coping strategies and work on ridding myself of harmful habits, like smoking and alcohol. My parents were so proud of me for quitting cigarettes they decided to buy me a gym membership at Square One. Lewis was my personal trainer and probably one of the most handsome men I have ever met. There was also a benevolence about him. One day, I was changing in the dressing room at the gym. I woman I knew from the facility stopped to ask me the following question, "Cheryl, you and Anne (an alternate trainer) have been friends for years. Why would you choose Lewis over Anne as your trainer?"

I asked her, "Have you had a really good look at Lewis lately? He's the person I want to look at when I'm struggling to do a few more push-ups—nothing against Anne." The circle of woman around us burst into fierce laughter.

Driving for the hospital and progressing from personal to business to insurance to transport clients had been a process. In my third year of driving, accident-free, my insurer gave me a very reasonable quote for business insurance to transport clients. It was a great moment of victory for me. The first client I transported, I took to a probation appointment. He slept all the way there. When I reported this, at Rounds, one of my colleagues shouted above the laughter, "You must be a great driver if they *sleep* in your car!"

The pleasure of my days was so often tied to our clients and my work on the ACT Team as case manager with a specialty in peer support. I remained uncertain as to whether kindness or acceptance was what they needed most. I was delighted by the sheer uniqueness of each person I served. Despite what I heard of their diagnosis, disability, and sometimes problematic behaviours, I spent a lot of time with clients—waxing philosophical, sharing the good and the bad, offering a lot of reassurance and support, and helping them get things like eyeglasses, new clothes, or a better level of fitness. On the team, I was especially trusted by these individuals so much so there was a joke once saying the team would create a life-size cutout of me should they refuse to meet with a colleague. When the laughter died down, another professional added, "And we need to record your voice!"

I know I am both a client and a professional, but in my heart, when I speak to a client, *I am one of them*. I really admire these people because I know what survival takes. They have all suffered greatly, dealt with it in one way or another, and keep trying without giving up. As one nurse with Mountridge General Hospital's day treatment program told us in group one day, "You are all my heroes."

Reassurances *like this* are vital because many mental health clients have trust and trauma issues. Also, the incredible suffering in mental illness is not publically recognized, documented, or understood. Survival takes persistence and great courage.

It was well-known at work that I was able to engage very challenging individuals as well as those very inhibited and withdrawn. It was not rocket science. It was the funnelling of compassion. It was wishing from somewhere deep, deep within to make a difference. I believe my own story made me especially sensitive to other people's vulnerabilities, and my vulnerabilities (like a ready transparency) allowed me to reach other people's unpleasant symptoms and emotions in a healing way.

Now

Now,
I forgive of myself,
my human vulnerability.
Within my mind,
the uncertainties
are like multidimensional objects,
and I am pressed for time.

When words fly,
reactions are fast.
Considerate words I have heard
from another room,
I repeat calmly to myself—
like prayers.
Sometimes,
I feel I will fly,
but I fall instead.
Sometimes,
I feel I will fall,
but I fly instead.
Better to embrace my illusions,
my delusions, my conclusions,
and other psychoses.
Important to stay in touch
with life contradictions—
I being one of them.

(Cheryl Yarek, Best Poets of 2014, Eber & Wein Publishing)

Coping

"I hate what life did to you, all the hurts and the disappointments, and the traumas, but *I love the person it made you become.*"

My cousin, CE in 2009

At the age of sixty, I remain convinced that *what we believe possible* is far stronger in determining our future than even reality. Forgiveness is a huge issue in mental health—not so much the ability to forgive others but the most difficult ability—the ability to forgive *oneself.* I wrote on Facebook, "I do not enjoy suffering, but it has taught me far more than every peaceful, contented, or joyful moment in my life combined." I have tried, partly, to live life as though it were an adventure. I believe that even a ton of sorrow, if you allow it, if you permit it, may eventually bring you the world's *greatest* treasures.

In speaking of coping, I do want to mention *counselling* because I have been receiving some my entire adult life. I have also been doing therapy for others—the people who could not make it there—always for the same reason: "I'm not crazy." To my credit, whenever I am crazy, *I know I am crazy* and seek help immediately!

I would very much caution you not to panic when terrible things take place in your life. Some of the worst things later can turn out to be some of the best things. My father's illness permitted the complete resolution of problems we faced together all our lives. Being fired from a job I valued opened the door to the dream job of my career. Turning dead-end pronouncements into victorious beginnings has been one positive statement of my career.

If I have learned anything, I have learned about what it is to be human and exceedingly vulnerable. This connects us when nothing else does. As a person with a bipolar diagnosis, I have a unique set of problems. Things are often very good or very bad, and sometimes, I do not want to be here. I have had to teach myself what to hang on to. It's God first, and often, it's God last.

It's also *always* other people. In the most sacred, special way, it's the clients I've known. If suspecting crisis, professionals ask: "Are you planning on killing yourself?" My response for the past twenty-seven years has been, "I can't possibly do that. I'm a client *and* a mental health professional. When I am well, I teach others about why they should live. If I take my own life, it's the greatest betrayal because it makes all my words, all my support, all my directives a bunch of bologna."

For me, survival is all about those people who love me and keep reaching out to me and handing me a lifeline in one form or another, whether we breakfast and walk together or line-dance at church, or like angels, they sometimes tolerate my upsets and my ranting. It's the professionals who have temporarily waived fees or read and reread drafts of this book on their personal time to offer feedback. In colloquial terms, I mean true-blue friends.

As a coping strategy, I offer you my six concepts:

a) Time as an ally
b) Therapy as the centre
c) Affirming relationships
d) Diagnosis as a tool
e) A give-and-take attitude
f) Facing fears

Time is the healer in a faster-and-faster-paced society. It is important to extend patience to *yourself* and forgiveness too. Recognize and deal with any fears around a relapse. What can you put into place right now? Time brought me many things—a diagnosis, supports, and a therapeutic relationship with my psychiatrist. Remember that recovery is really a lifelong process.

At the very least, it helps to recognize sometimes that "It's probably never going to be as bad as it was."

Psychiatry and therapy propelled me forward. In preparing for sessions, I would ask myself, "What is the main issue at this time?" I also needed to identify and locate any area of discomfort and the level or degree of that discomfort. Sometimes, there were several issues. I needed then to prioritize or create a therapy to-do list. (I would take this paperwork to my session as a reminder.)

In the beginning, accepting positive people into my life and affirming relationships was something I needed more awareness around. First, I needed to feel worthy of positive attention. I also needed to feel safe. I learned that I actually had a "right" to my thoughts and feelings. Sometimes, I would choose the familiar even when the familiar was inappropriate for me. The first fully affirming relationship I had was with my therapist. (This was an important education to receive.)

A diagnosis is a way to establish an area or areas of vulnerability and sensitivity. Also, in my view, the diagnosis addresses what needs to be addressed. Getting a diagnosis changed my life for the better. My preference remains for my life after my diagnosis rather than life before my diagnosis. It sounds strange, but I liked getting it! Finally, we had something to call this!

If you adopt an attitude of "give and take," this helps to establish gratitude. I feel there is much to be grateful for and perhaps a debt to be paid *for the gift of a sound mind.* I am often reminded of my mother's favourite expression: "There is nothing so bad that something good does not come of it."

I learned, especially in group work at my client hospital, that sharing feelings of anger, sadness, fear, disillusionment, and anxiety were the beginning of personal empowerment. Sometimes we feel alone when we are not in fact alone. To admit that you fear is exactly what helps to remove the fear. It also provides you with perspective. Gaining perspective is the main goal of therapy because when I can do that, I can begin to "manage" my life.

Public speaking, became for me, another way of coping. I became an advocate for the advancement of the mental health cause with a strong desire to provide those affected, (through professional venues) with openness and comfort. From 1997-2010, I made 19-Mental Health Presentations; two were at major conferences. I then joined "Toastmasters" in my community. My first speech was at the Mississauga Library location. I received the following feedback:

a) Wonderful—loved it. Well organized, inspirational, and easy to follow. Keep up the good work!

b) Very well done. Little bit of movement and taking out the lectern could help improve.

c) Excellent speech. You met all the objectives of the speech.

d) Great way of tying your father's story to your theme. A bit of humour in second story kept us interested. Be careful with "hum."

e) Very relevant to the topic. Very well organized. Three good examples. I like the sense of humour in your presentation.

f) Very nice structure to your speech. Your speaking voice is very personable. The subject matter was well-chosen. Loved it!

g) Very good personal references. Though a serious topic, you had some humour. Great conclusion.

h) So inspiring. Thank you for sharing your love of God. Very well organized as well.

i) I enjoyed your speech for learning lots of tips we should be aware of in our life.

j) Great title and great topic! I found it to be creative. Next time, try to get away from lectern to gesture your examples. Watch the use of "um." I really loved your speech! Inspirational.

In mental health, I hope we can lead others to their power by inspiring hope, celebrating honesty, and acknowledging courage. Let's provide comfort in the face of fear and acceptance in the face of judgement. Let's explore and share the challenges and rewards inherent in the recovery process.

Helping other people remains a huge re-enforcer for me. It highlights and explains and makes sense of my continuing good fortune. For example, one fellow asks for change outside the corner store. I dig in my purse and give him some money. Once in the store, I shop for my items, including several cans of cold pop. As I leave the store, he is still outside. I put my bag on the ground and say, "It's hot out. Would you like a Coke Zero, an ice tea, or a ginger ale?" He is slow to decide. I believe it may be because he has forgotten what it is like to have the luxury of *choice*. He picks the ice tea but cannot disguise his shock with me while I think, *Is there a reason why we are not better to one another?* (Why be annoyed that someone is asking? It is much wiser to remain grateful that you are in a position to give!)

In relation to this, the coping strategy I have utilized the very most in recovery is gratitude. I have written hundreds of thank-you cards or letters. I was taught in childhood that you need to formally thank people since no one is obligated to assist you, and when they do, it is healing to acknowledge the support. (Once, I even received a thank-you note in response to my thank-you letter! I had expressed appreciation to Jack McClelland—from McClelland & Stewart Publishing—for an interview he provided.)

One thank-you letter to my psychiatrist reads as follows:

Dear Dr. Marie Philips,

You cannot possibly comprehend the extent to which your assistance has both enabled me and continues to propel me forward. Even in the flashing seconds of my complete insecurity, the bond I share with you disengages my past propensity to despair. If the English language were what prevented me from describing succinctly my feelings, I would learn a second tongue. I do know, even as a writer, that words can never quite embrace the soul of my feelings for you any more than I can raise my arm and touch the sky.

I need to let you know that, yes, I notice things. I am constantly aware of how you continue to persist to make my life better, to make situations work. They say, "Go the extra mile." You are the expression personified. Sometimes it seems there is little you would not do for me. Understand I remember both the small and the grand gestures.

I feel as though I have been able to step confidently over the most insurmountable obstacles with your wise counsel at every turn. Interestingly enough, the more of your humanness I uncover, the more you matter to me. Now that I have made you laugh so hard you cried, I feel as powerful as the crickets announcing the fall of tonight.

Cheryl

Reaching

Sometimes I feel from you—
all the things you do not say.
Your hands reach out
and touch my humanity.
I reach back—
amid the broken pieces of my life—
do my very best to make
a bouquet for you.

(Cheryl Yarek, Best Poets of 2015, Eber & Wein Publishing)

Humour remains one of the best ways to cope. I wrote the following comedy routine to explain my position as a new driver at the age of forty-three:

Why does everyone ask, "Why are you afraid to drive?" You must be kidding! What a stupid question. I'm afraid to drive because somebody could get hurt! My instructor told me I asked interesting questions like, "How much does a car weigh?" The answer? "A few tons." Here I am behind the wheel of "a few tons," and basically, I haven't a clue what I am doing. Piece it together, folks. DANGER. When I was learning to drive, there was way too much going on. It made me nervous. One of my friends suggested, "Maybe take a tranquilizer before driving." She knows some people who do *that*! Wow. Now I'm *really* scared. I tried to narrow down the things to focus on while driving . . . tried to focus on the gas and brake. Problem was sometimes I confused the two! My uncle says to me, "That's how people get killed!" Wow. I knew *that*. What separates a new and experienced driver?

Nothing more than a yellow light. When I was a new driver, I stopped for them all even if that meant squealing the tires and maybe scaring people. Now? I *never* stop for an amber light. Amber means accelerator to the floor, and look around a lot while praying!

I will conclude my "Coping" chapter with this:

Things I Thought about While in the Arms of My Church

Please, God, continue to lead me in the best directions to do Your will, find true happiness, and proclaim Your Word.

Please help me always to stay true to You although Your plans may seem inconvenient compared to my own. Although we live in a microwave society, help me to spend the time to get to know other people, and let it never be said by anyone that they spoke to me but walked away feeling unheard.

God, let me know my place, realizing there are both people better at some things and not as proficient at others. Let me never believe that any of this makes me better or worse or less or more loved by God.

Help me to be encouraging and enthusiastic without pushing people. Let my life be an example of good values composed of both my successes and my failures. Help me to teach how falling down is not about lying down but rising up! Give me some nuggets of wisdom to share with others as when Evelyn, on the church bus trip, recommended sliced cucumber for rising blood pressure!

God, let me never ever, ever be unteachable. Let me never ever, ever turn my back on another human being when I myself have been taught and have been shown mercy. Let me never believe that I was asked to determine someone's worthiness. Let me continue to give loonies and toonies to the homeless who wait for me along my route.

Help me to realize that it's not about anything but the blood of Jesus, and love and truth, and kindness and faith, and having integrity. Let me learn Your lessons, such as laughter is contagious and clearly a disease worth catching. Or if you would like to grab someone's attention, try it with manners and respect.

Thank you, God, for sending others stronger and wiser to teach me about loving myself and especially forgiving myself before Your eyes and through Your mercy.

(Written by Cheryl Yarek on June 13, 2010, during a church trip to Quebec City, Canada.)

EAP—Employee Assistance Program

"You are a force to be reckoned with!"

My counsellor, 2011

Wayne Fielding was my first counsellor at EAP. He gave me two assignments immediately. The first was to write down ten positive qualities about myself. The second assignment was asking myself that if I was able to change my circumstances and remove challenges, what would I want my life to look like? How would all this change the feelings I have about myself?

The positive qualities I cited were the following:

1. I am very passionate about everything; I do nothing in a half-measured way.
2. When we go through the fire together, I will support and love you indefinitely.
3. I am an extremely good writer, but first, I was an avid reader.
4. I am loved for my cooking and baking.
5. I will do everything I can think of to help a client and team members say the clients know it.
6. I am very ethical. I also teach it and live it.
7. I am courageous, intuitive, and creative.
8. I am practical and try to use my learning and sometimes my suffering to make the world better.

9. I am active mentally and physically.
10. I am appreciative—e.g., when I received the position with ACTT, I sent all three of my female references a floral bouquet.

In counselling with Wayne, I also created some prose called "My Insecurity." Wayne said he was having problems understanding why, with my experience and gifts, I would have *any* security issues. To explain, I wrote the following:

My Insecurity

The root of my insecurity is this;
I have suffered the greatest loss imaginable to
human kind—I have lost my mind.
The fact that I can recall the impact of
madness, like it happened yesterday,
is why some say I am an incredible worker,
and yet this ability to help remains
a double-edged sword.
Mine has been a life of extremes,
and I imagine always will be.
However, understand I do not mean
to state this—unhappily.

(Cheryl Yarek, 2007)

Wayne had focused time and energy trying to convince me to stop *any* alcohol use because of my medications. I was a very moderate drinker, but Wayne insisted this still affected me in a very negative way because I took medications. Hearing all this, I decided that day to begin an experiment—to prove him wrong. My plan was I would stop all alcohol use immediately for two months. Once I could prove that the removal of the substance made no difference whatsoever, I would share the experiment and the results with him. I was convinced that he would be wrong, wrong, wrong.

We continued our regular appointments, and exactly two months later, I sat in his office, telling him about planning the experiment to "prove you wrong." He smiled. I let him know the results were in, and I was completely mistaken—the experiment proved him completely right, not wrong. I realized, soon enough, that even a moderate amount of alcohol had had a negative impact on my cognition. Stopping its use completely had permitted me to improve my thinking significantly. Things were much clearer, and I was never ever happier with my thought processes.

My counselling relationship with Wayne became complicated (I was unable to continue) because I developed a huge crush on him. I was enamoured with his conservative style; I think it was his intelligence but also very much his spotless shoes and his cashmere sweaters. I hadn't cried much since 1998 until I started meeting with him in that office off Hurontario Street. I have truly had great hardships in life, but I have also had enormous opportunities. I believe that meeting Wayne was one of those significant opportunities. (I ended counselling with him and would follow up by email in 2011.)

Anne-Marie became my second EAP counsellor. We discussed Wayne, and she said, "Some relationships cannot be resolved in person."

"You know," I remarked, "this is a case of therapy-causing-therapy." We both laughed and laughed. I even brought an art piece I had made Wayne to a session with Anne-Marie. "It's happy," she acknowledged, "full of hope." Later, I would destroy the piece. It hung on my wall too long, holding me hostage to a past that I permitted to hurt me over and over again like a compulsion. My dismantling of the art piece was my refusal to choose the past over the present—one minute longer.

Anne-Marie was the epitome of kindness and empathy. She was a huge source of *comfort* to me whenever I sensed the presence of hostility around me. Anne-Marie and our counseling together began sometime in late 2007, early 2008. The first letter I wrote her begins, "I would like to be writing about achieving perfection as a human being. However, that's not actually the case." The correspondence continues, "I do think of you guys (EAP) often, *brag* to others about your abilities, competencies, and general brilliance at every possible opportunity. I have never met a team of people quite like you. This is very much why I admire and love you all so much. You have not only helped me to hold on to work I simply love; you have taught me how to grow stronger and happier and wiser and more capable and positive. Wow."

I spoke to Anne-Marie about the fact that I had learned far more in my EAP sessions than about "anger." In terms of anger, I learned to become more "aware" first, then to modify my thinking. I also learned a lot about what makes successful relationships. I told Anne-Marie that I was working at my dream job.

"Do they expect a lot?" I asked her.

"Well, yes," I answered myself, "but perhaps that is the price you pay for a dream job!"

In early 2008, I was having problems letting go of the past. Anne-Marie asked me how I felt it interfered. I explained that there seemed to be numerous people who remembered what happened to me during my first mental illness episode even better than I did. And these people seemed intent on nailing me to the cross of my past.

Few people seem to know that mental illness is genetic. My life had unfolded back then like a series of betrayals, and as I dealt with the stigma and cruelty of some people, I was left to feel like human garbage—completely disposable. I also learned from the experience that if you do not know who you are and what you believe in, there are many who will happily decide these things for you. One woman even insisted I was sexually abused as a child. (I was not.) Her stance, however, seemed vital to her because it would permit us to be victims together.

In March 2008, I mailed a thank-you letter to their office titled "EAP: To People Impossible to Forget." It expressed appreciation for the teaching of self-respect and self-nurturing and provided thanks for the acknowledgement of personal courage. I not only had two excellent counsellors whom I saw at their offices, I also received telephone counselling from EAP numerous times. The letter also detailed the help I got in crisis when I was dealing with the upcoming appointment with my manager to discuss my supervisor. The previous day, team members had been shaking my hand and telling me they had "enjoyed" working with me. When I was puzzled, the response was, "Nobody reports their supervisor to their manager."

In speaking to Deanna at EAP by phone and outlining the matter, she asked a simple question of me, "Cheryl, what choice do you have?"

My reply was, "I have no choice."

"You're right," she assured.

Throughout the discussion, I could not stop pacing. As our interaction concluded, Deanna had practical advice. She suggested some light exercise at the apartment gym, a shower, and a herbal tea. I slept deeply and soundly that night. This would have been an absolute impossibility without her intervention.

In my thank-you letter to them, I added the following, "Because of your understanding and caring, I take risks I would be too afraid to take otherwise. They are not careless risks. They are risks about taking the chance that I matter, that I can effect positive change, that one person can change circumstances in an important way for themselves and others. You have *never* treated me like a disabled person although I have bipolar. You have treated me like an extremely capable and intelligent person. And bless you because in the process I have become one! In all seriousness, I have been treated by EAP like gold, and this has made me realize that no one should treat me in a shabby way. I wish I could come over there and HUG you all!"

In 2009, I thanked Anne-Marie for "teaching me how important, how brilliant, and how capable I am." Her dedication and honesty took me so many places I needed to go, including back to childhood. I wrote to her, "In order to negotiate the darkness and the despair, I held onto in memory, your every word and those words were like hands guiding me back down, into the black hole, and later pulling me back to the surface. In the process, I became stronger and have come to know confidence in a way I never imagined for myself." As a gesture of appreciation, I gave Anne-Marie the best book I have ever read on recovery, *Healing from Trauma* by Jasmin Lee Cori. (I have read more than one hundred books related to aspects of mental health recovery.)

My family wished to encourage me in writing my story, this book. So years ago, my mother financed a new computer for me, and my technology-savvy brother, programmed it. More recently, my mother noted, "We did everything we could think of to help, but it wasn't until Anne-Marie at EAP started reading your book that you even got serious."

In 2011, as I mentioned, I followed up with Wayne by email. I explained why I had ended counselling with him four years earlier: I had realized my feelings were "inappropriate." Ending this professional relationship was extremely difficult for me, but as I wrote, "It is common for the difficult path to be thrust upon me." I also wrote, "I would like you to know how much my life changed through the time I spent in counselling with you. You gave me such strength and resolve. The right energy and the right ideas move through me in a certain way, because of you. I have always been somewhat confident, but you helped to make me unstoppable. Ending our connection hurt so much but was a match for the lessons I learned from you about being strong, remaining courageous, never pretending, and loving with everything I have within my person. Still, I make mistakes. More than once, I have said to my family, 'Yes, there are times I am *very stupid* for a genius girl.'"

I had one friend who thought I was very conceited to fall for Wayne Fielding, and she wished to argue about it. I stopped calling or meeting with her. One day, following a year of silence, she telephoned. She asked me to take up boxing with her—something she felt she excelled at. I naively agreed to box with her and never heard from her again. (She weighed about 350 pounds.) In telling this story to a friend, the following thought registered, "What if her plan was to meet with me for boxing and kick the crap out of me?" My friend and I roared and roared with laughter, and Anita said, "I guess you called her bluff!"

Outside of the War

You begin each day with my love,
as round as a promise, as collected as a sigh.
It unwinds, it unfolds, it shines
. . . yellow.
My loving you has nothing to with
with sweetheart roses.
It has to do with
your taking me
outside of the war.
As long as you are
somewhere in the world,
I live with perfect security.
And everything you win
is part of my victory.
For you are
the amazing language I meant to speak.
For you are
the revolution I meant to start

(Cheryl Yarek, Poetry Toronto, 1980)

Medication Toxic and
the Middle East

"You might not live long enough to make it to Mountridge
General. We are driving across the street to Trillium."

My mother, May 2011

I went on a trip to Israel and Egypt with my church in the early
summer of 2011. My friends later said I was already ill for a
period of many months before departure. They noted more
impatience and what seemed like stress issues. Still, no one was overly
worried because I was scheduled to see Dr. Philips, who knew my
plans to go overseas. During the appointment, however, Dr. Philips
expressed no concerns whatsoever about my pending trip, although
by the time I left Canada, I had deteriorated physically and mentally
in a significant way. My body shook uncontrollably at times, and one
of the church members asked loudly on the bus, "Are you a retard? Is
that why you shake like that?" A number of members were intensely
cruel and mean. No one at any point during the excursion asked me
if I might need any medical help or assistance. One woman sprained
her ankle while we were in Israel. She was later told that they expected
her to participate in all the outings because as the leader noted, "That
is what you signed up for." (I remember hoping my world somehow
wouldn't actually stay this way.) I was approached soon after by Irene,
who asked me to sit with her and three of her friends. These women
were kind and considerate throughout. (Irene and I are friends to
this day.)

I returned to work from the Middle East completely out of sorts.

It was one of my clients who expressed concern and suggested an immediate visit to my family physician. Startled, she remarked, "Your whole body is jumping." I called my supervisor and told her I needed to visit my doctor.

I saw my family doctor, and she ordered blood work. Then she could not get in touch with me. My hand tremors were extremely serious; my fingers were jumping and leaping out of control. I could not even dial a telephone because my fingers did not rest on any numbers long enough. I was in my apartment, trapped. My thinking was muddled. I tried to organize and clean the place, not even imaging that medically I was close to death. My mother did not hear from me and appeared at my apartment door. Taking one look at me, she said, "Where's your health card? You're going to hospital." I tried to explain that going across the street to Trillium was a conflict of interest and that she needed to drive me to Mountridge General Hospital, where I was a client. She made clear that "you might not live long enough to make it to Mountridge General. We are driving across the street to Trillium." (I began a sick leave from work on May 17, 2011, that would last for two and one-half years.)

My recollection of hospital is sketchy; it comes back to me like a puzzle in pieces. I was waiting in emergency with my mother for six to seven hours. We were in an examining room when I lost all the patience I had left and decided to let the staff know I am leaving. They would not allow this and paged a doctor, who saw me after a review of my blood levels.

"You are a very sick girl," he conveyed. "The normal level for the medication in the blood is around 1.1, and your level is 5.7." He and I talked, and he prevented my mother from interrupting by respectfully whispering, "Shhhh . . ." to her. He looked at me, and there was kindness in his eyes. I mention this because I was seriously alarmed and looking for a positive to hang on to.

They were transporting me to ICU. (My mother later told me when she saw me there, she felt they had found every piece of equipment they could uncover in the hospital and attached it to me.) At one point, they were putting tubing inside me. The nurse was gentle and had compassion. The room was quiet, undisturbed by her busyness.

Next, I was on a bed, literally flying down the hospital corridor, and the doctor was shouting, "Take out the tubing! Give her oxygen! Get her to X-ray!" I began to pray, asking God *not* to take me because I was so shocked He was considering this. "You cannot possibly take me now!" I shouted out loud. "I have done every single thing You asked me to! I haven't even been married yet!" This was my last remark before the darkness descended for days.

I woke up in ICU, convinced I was on a spaceship. I had never seen any place like it. (Woke up on Mars?) I saw a doctor and told him I was very, very hungry. I asked him if I might have an egg salad sandwich. He smiled. "I will *personally* go and get you an egg salad sandwich," he replied. Staff appeared delighted that I had regained consciousness.

One of the emergency doctors saw me and told me they were very concerned because the level of medication in the blood was so high. They took me to a room in the geriatric section of Mental Health, where the other emergency doctor appeared while I was walking the hall in circles for exercise. He touched my right arm and smiled. He now seemed pleased with the day, with me, and with himself.

Medication was discussed with me. They wanted me to take the same medication again, because of my positive track record with it. I refused. They pushed. "Try dying first!" I exclaimed. "Then *you* take it!" They stopped pushing and chose a different mood stabilizer. The level of any existing medication in my blood along with the new mood stabilizer would make me look mad. I had never heard of this possible side effect in my career. One day, I caught my eye in the mirror with horror. I scared me!

Upon discharge, I coped by writing ten positives about my situation:

a)   God is in charge, and He will never leave or forsake me.
b)   I have a job and can determine my needs.
c)   I have shelter, food, family, friends, and a church.

d)   I can pray, dance, shout, and cry.

e)   I express myself well—verbally and in writing.

f)   Everything is a learning situation.

g)   I know people with good ideas.

h)   I will receive benefits soon.

i)   I have savings.

j)   I can volunteer at church.

I was eventually discharged home with a personal support worker visiting occasionally. Soon after, my friend Margo called about going for coffee. I asked her if she could drive me to Mountridge General, instead. I had been in the apartment building all day (where many children live), and I heard what sounded like gunfire coming from the parking lot. I was completely unaware that it was Canada Day and the explosions were fireworks. Soon after discharge from Trillium, I was now back in hospital—at Mountridge General. I was very ill and very bored in hospital. I noticed that some patients had written on the walls of the room. I decided to be less obvious. I wrote about God on the wall in the closet.

My words were, "The will of God will never take you where the grace of God will not protect you."

My brother had given me this, and I loved it. The next day, Dr. Richards walked into my room and immediately went to the closet, throwing the door open. "Did you write this?" he demanded, obviously offended.

"This is the crazy house," I informed him. "That is what we do here, write on walls."

He asked me to come to the window. I stood beside him. "When you look out the window, you see the same things I do," he remarked. "You see a road, and trees, and the sky."

"We don't see the same thing!" I raged. "Of course, we do," he insisted.

"The difference is," I shouted, "you have the key to the damn front door, and I don't!" Dr. Richards left. He'll be back tomorrow to argue again, I mused.

I was so bored that I was constantly on the phone in the corridor. I didn't have any money. The phone was free, and they let me keep my address book. I decided to call my former lawyer who helped with my separation from Louis to say hello and let him know I was in hospital. His secretary asked who was calling and how I knew her employer. I replied, "We know each other from a 1998 out-of-court settlement called *Yarek vs. Louis's mother.*" The lawyer returned my call that evening and spent considerable time on the phone, permitting me to vent.

Next, I left him a voice mail asking for an important delivery in person. My exact words were, "If you are stopping by the area anytime from 2:00 to 8:00 p.m., each day, I could use Scope—the green one—spearmint. Thanks." Then I left him the number for my voice mail. I know from notes I kept then that I called him quite a few times. He was always tolerant, kind, a gentleman. One of my nurses later remarked, "You are hilarious when you are ill. We are always amazed by this incredible humour in the midst of your illness."

I decided to call the police about the church I had attended and gone with to the Middle East—file a report from the hospital. I said the following, "This is Cheryl Yarek, Roman's daughter. He worked for the sheriff's department in Ontario until his death nine years ago. I would appreciate the police undercover investigating a church I belonged to for the past one and a half years." I then left my telephone number. Constable Miller responded. He left this voice mail and advice: "Cheryl, stop going to the church."

I started to worry about work—one of my colleagues in particular—and the clients. God answered me with the following words, which I wrote down, "Don't be a hero. People would not speak for you or for themselves. Don't speak now for them. God is righteous and good, and He will see your case through. We get what we deserve in the end. Actually, no one is fooling anyone about anything any of the time" (July 22, 2011).

I spoke to Occupational Health at work, and they recommended I go to the Centre for Addiction and Mental Health (CAMH) for an assessment since I was refusing to see Dr. Philips. I went to CAMH by transit but became distracted by the intensity of construction work there, the displays, and the clients. I was having far too much fun to worry or ponder about being assessed. Reality only hit me as I exited onto the street hours later.

I decided to return to my former psychiatrist (on July 27, 2011) after a fifty-seven-dollar cab ride from CAMH to her office. I was dealing with a lot of fears. (I had put in a call to a medical clinic in Etobicoke in December 2010, asking for help in finding a new psychiatrist but would wait one year for my request to be completed.) In the meantime, I questioned my psychiatrist's abilities. Despite numerous opportunities, she never ever acknowledged her mistake or any error in my care. Once, she even asked me, "Have you ever been arrested?" I considered this a bizarre question when I had been in therapy with her for almost three decades. Her lack of remorse and caring were concerning. Once, when I was in tears over missing my job and the clients, she looked at me and asked, "Do you know how pathetic you sound?"

I saw her frequently but did not find her help helpful. One day, she said to me, "I don't know what to do to help you. What do *you* think we should do?" I said I thought she should refer me to Day Treatment so that I would have more interactions and a schedule. She seemed surprised that I wanted this, but she made the referral. Day Treatment groups were a challenge for me. I suspected that complaining about my psychiatrist, Dr. Philips, at Mountridge General would not bear fruit, so I focused on my other issues. I very much needed the help I was receiving, after all. Eventually, the situation was resolved when I received a call from the medical clinic in Etobicoke and was given an initial appointment on December 12, 2011, with a psychiatrist there.

Meanwhile, I discovered a coffee shop in West Toronto that became my favorite. There were tons of comfy chairs. The manager there served me once then seemed afraid of me there ever after. I knew it was my "mad eyes." I was *very* affected by the notion that someone was afraid of me. What could I possibly say to him: "It's really OK, I'm perfectly harmless. My meds just give me this crazed look?"

Dr. Jay, my new psychiatrist at the medical clinic, asked me if I would accept a consulting referral to a psychiatrist at Sunnybrook

Health Centre. I was so honoured she would even think of this way of helping. I said yes. The day of the appointment, the secretary called, and I confirmed that I would be there, adding, "I don't drive anymore, so my mom will bring me."

She asked, "Can the doctor interview her as well?"

"Sure," I replied without thinking.

When I mentioned this to my mother, she was very hesitant. We agreed the psychiatrist might interview us together but that she didn't want to be seen by him alone. Once there, my mom changed her mind. He was very respectful, and we were both happy. His first question to me, he said, was to clarify. "You have bipolar and have worked on an ACT team for twelve years?"

"Yes," I replied.

He found this unbelievable. "Do you know what those ACTT jobs are called?" he enquired.

"No," I replied.

"They're called pressure-cooker jobs," he explained.

The Sunnybrook psychiatrist and Dr. Jay were reassuring, so I decided to return to taking my previous medication, the one whose escalating level had sent me to emergency. They were right—it was the medication that I have had the most positive history with. Dr. Jay promised frequent blood monitoring—every month.

It is largely unknown that episodes involving mental illness take many years to resolve—not days or months. It therefore took a very long time for me to try to negotiate this recovery piece. I was caught up in memories surrounding almost dying and partly where to place blame. (Before becoming ill, the level of medication in my blood had not been checked for eleven months.) Everyone but me believed I should sue. (Even my mother insisted on this route.) I could not, though, because this was the same professional who helped me recover from psychotic depression, who was patient, and wise, and fair for decades. I decided not to sue my psychiatrist because of my conscience.

From childhood, the church taught me this measure. You act according to what is right—the language your heart speaks. A lawsuit seemed wrong for every reason. Mostly, I understood you do not repay phenomenal caring, support, healing, and inspiration with this type of response. If I had never met this particular psychiatrist, I would never have been motivated to emulate her as a professional in mental health, and my career has meant everything to me. Also, I am an Ontario resident with OHIP health coverage. In my first recovery, I had been given the opportunity to heal without the financial burden of hospital bills for days admitted and therapy given. And some people don't want to even pay hospital parking because it's expensive! *Please*, folks!

I prayed to ask God how to heal, how to negotiate this part. He said, paraphrasing, "Yes. It was bad, very bad. But what I want you to do to heal now is to stop focusing on that and start to focus on all the *amazing people* I will be sending your way to help you recover. Cheryl, thank those people. Consider this to be *payback time*. Get those prayers out there and those thank-you notes. This is the path to full healing."

One day, I was saying prayers in the prayer room (sacred space) at Trillium Mississauga (I lived across the street) and realized there were no tissues there. I decided to begin to stock the prayer room regularly with two boxes of Kleenex—one for the Muslim individuals and one for the Christians.

I was informed that the severity of the damage done by a medication level almost six times what is normal was yet to await me. The medical predictions were severe mental and physical impairments. I started the next leg of "that possible journey" by walking to the prayer room at Trillium to write in the prayer book and to pray.

I started by praying for the professionals who have loved and supported me, my dear friends, and loving family, and for the safety of everyone working at the hospital, putting a white light around each of them. I then asked God for His help in providing a full healing as He had indicated. Then like my dad, I ended that day's prayer with the words, "Thank you, God. Thanks for another day of living."

Map to the Uneven Fire

Our laughter is a waltz
that breaks the mimicry of silence,
a compromise, a solace,
to the dance steps of the sky.
Don't expect me to stay
head to head,
looking at the night
when I trust you to build
with many small sticks—
even the moon.

(Cheryl Yarek, Poetry Toronto, 1980)

With Appreciation
from the Author

"A successful woman is one who can build a firm foundation
even from the bricks others have thrown at her."

Unknown

I would like to thank my country, Canada, for the honour of being born here with a sense of humour and a full head of hair. Thank you for being a land of safety nets and opportunities. Thank you for being a country of diversity in language and culture. Thanks for being rich in caring. Thank you for providing programs like Self-Employment Assistance, Psychology of Achievement, and Humber College's Job Finding Club. Thank you for supporting me through my most difficult periods with welfare and the Ontario Disability Support Program. Thank you for incredible hospitals and mental health agencies that help so many, especially Family Association for Mental Health Everywhere, the Mood Disorders Association, the distress lines, and the public libraries where I borrowed books and researched my issues for free. My special thanks to emergency services—police, ambulance, and fire—for hearing me, serving me with compassion, and ensuring my safety in my most terrifying hours. I need to extend my thanks also to those who operate the transit system in the Greater Toronto Area. Once during my illness, a driver permitted me to pay the full fare in pennies. Another driver agreed to transport me for free because I gave my word I would pay two tickets the next time. Thank you, Canada, and God forever bless you for believing so strongly in your people.

Success is never ever, ever, ever about one person. I would like to thank the following people who threw no bricks: Dr. Marie Philips, who directed and guided me out of a psychological wilderness; my family doctor for her sincerity and dedication and her secretary for always making it happen; Dr. Ryan Forbes, who could not have been more kind in the early days of my professional learning; Dr. Jay, who encouraged me with, "Cheryl, you have a direct line to God," and especially, especially because she considered the learning in therapy to be reciprocal. I would like to acknowledge the rescue by the two emergency physicians at Trillium who saved my life following an enormously elevated medication level, and with great kindness, handed my life back to me. There is no truly effective thank you. Special appreciation to Dr. Head, who sat with me in hospital each day. Calm would descend literally each time he entered the room. Thanks also to Dr. Richards for his caring and concern.

I would also like to mention Reverend Smith, who found my views very interesting and often called on me to express them; Pastor Karen Milley, who met with me to be supportive and to share our love of Joyce Meyer; Reverend Ed Clements, who put a great deal of energy into helping me deal with my past and did this so effectively—I forgave myself those transgressions. (Twenty-seven years of therapy touched them but did not clear them.) I want to thank the Roman Catholic priest who, when I appeared at the rectory door asking to be blessed, simply blessed me. Thanks to Sister Helen at Loretto Brunswick College School, who spent hours and hours hearing me out and wisely and with great laughter redirected me from joining the nunnery.

I would like to thank my friends: Robert for his twenty-eight-year commitment to talking on the phone every weekend and Frank for his support and thoughtfulness and being the very finest Bible class teacher I will ever know! I also would like to thank Elvita for her strength, Irene for her tenacity and for praying such gorgeous prayers over me, Deb for her energy and persistence and for being complimentary and observant, Al for covering my back, Dwight for encouraging me, David for his ready listening skills, Marthese for always being available through email, Elizabeth for her willingness to intervene anytime and forever in helpful ways, and Margaret for believing when I wasn't able to.

I would like to thank my family. Thanks to my maternal grandmother for covering the cost of my university education and therefore giving me great hope (when I had none) and showing great understanding and love. I would like to thank my maternal grandfather for his ambition and great financial success in farming, showing that anything is possible if you work hard enough and remain honest. I wish to mention my paternal grandparents and thank them for putting the positives about freedom and Canada into perspective for me my entire life and for sharing their deep respect and love for this country. I want to acknowledge my godfather Uncle Pete, who taught me to drive—late in life—when I was petrified to do so. Thanks to my godmother Mary Ann, who treated me like a second daughter, taking me into stores on my birthday with the remark, "Choose anything you like." I need and wish to thank my father for teaching me discipline and giving me passion for my work and, most importantly, for forcing me to go to church every Sunday for sixteen years. (Without faith, I simply would not be here.) I want to thank my mother for her ready support and for valuing personal choice and freedom; for permitting me to explore, discover, and fly; and for providing a safe spot to land whenever I crashed. I want to extend extensive thanks to my brother, Darrell, who is the only one who shares my childhood history. I thank you for always being there in the really important ways, such as insisting on checking my refrigerator for food and filling it with groceries. You have been and are my angel brother.

Talent or skills or gifts are meaningless without backing. I want to thank Trillium Health Partners for backing me and supporting my ideas for the many years I worked at Trillium. Thank you for empowering me to make a difference, for doing things like enriching my life in important ways, and once even saving it. *(You folks will always have my heart.)*

I would like to thank the reader for choosing this book. I hope its message reached you in a way that matters, making a positive difference in your life. Enjoy your week!